J. Anne Helgren

Abyssinian Cats

Everything About Acquisition, Care, Nutrition,
Behavior, Health Care, and Breeding

With 43 Color Photographs

Illustrations by Michele Earle-Bridges

BARRON'S

Dedication:
To my best friend, Bill Helgren, and to my writing buddy, Robin Montgomery, without whose loving help and support—well, YOU know.

All inquiries should be addressed to:
Barron's Educational Series, Inc.
250 Wireless Boulevard
Hauppauge, NY 11788

International Standard Book No. 0-8120-2864-3

Library of Congress Catalog Card No. 94-24764

Library of Congress Cataloging-in-Publication Data
Helgren, J. Anne.
    Abyssinian cats : everything about acquisition, care, nutrition, behavior, health care, and breeding / J. Anne Helgren ; illustrations by Michele Earle-Bridges.
        p.   cm.
        "Barron's pet owner's manual."
        Includes bibliographical references (p. 109) and index.
        ISBN 0-8120-2864-3
        1. Abyssinian cats. I. Title.
    SF449.A28H45   1995   94-24764
    636.8'26—dc20   CIP

Printed in Hong Kong

56789   9955   987654321

About the Author:
J. Anne Helgren is a contributing editor and writes the featured "Breed of the Month" column for *Cats Magazine.* She is a professional member of the Cat Writers' Association and has written dozens of articles on cats for national and regional magazines and newspapers. Helgren has a lifetime of experience with the feline species, including ten years with the Abyssinian breed, and has conducted extensive research on cat-related topics, including interviews with breeders, judges, fanciers, and veterinarians. She lives near Sacramento, California, with her husband, Bill, and two Abyssinian friends.

Photo Credits:
Mark McCullough (Through The Cat's Eye): front cover photo, inside front cover, rear cover photos, inside back cover. Photos on pages: 8, 9, 16, 17, 20, 33, 37, 40, 44, 45, 60, 61, 65, 80, 81, 85, 88, 89, 92, 96, 97, 101, 104, and 108.
    Penni Putman (24 KT Kats Abyssinians): photos on pages: 13, 48, and 56.
    J. Anne Helgren: photos on pages: 25, 28, 52, 57, 68, 77, and 105. Page 28 is of Leslie L.C. Burchfield's daughter Lauren and her blue Abyssinian Faberge. Page 68 is of JT's Cattery Abyssinians in their cat run.
    Tom Stewart and Jim Gawronski (JT's Cattery): photos on pages: 12, 24, 32, 53, 93, and 100.
    Tom Moss: photo on page 5.

Important Note:
When you handle cats, you may sometimes get scratched or bitten. If this happens, have a doctor treat the injuries immediately.
    Make sure your cat receives all the necessary shots and dewormings, otherwise serious danger to the animal and to human health may arise. A few diseases and parasites can be communicated to humans. If your cat shows any signs of illness, you should definitely consult a veterinarian. If you are worried about your own health, see your doctor and tell him or her that you have cats.
    Some people have allergic reactions to cats. If you think you might be allergic, see your doctor before you get a cat.
    It is possible for a cat to cause damage to someone else's property and even to cause accidents. For your own protection you should make sure your insurance covers such eventualities, and you should definitely have liability insurance.

Contents

Preface

Humans have been fascinated with the feline for as long as people and cats have shared this planet. The self-confidence of cats, the careful contemplation of the world around them, their shrewdness and individuality, those glowing eyes that seem to know more than they are willing to say—these qualities make cats an enigma that humankind for ages has struggled to comprehend.

The Abyssinian has all these qualities and more, and will appeal to the cat lover who wants a companion who is the epitome of the regal beauty and independent spirit of the feline.

I love all cats, but the Abyssinian will always have a special place in my heart. I fell in love with Abyssinians by accident—literally—at the first cat show I attended. Wandering in awe among cages of long, lanky Siamese, round, ornate Persians and other exotic felines, I heard a sudden cry of "Cat loose!" Out of nowhere, a ruddy streak shot past me, startling me into bumping one of the judges and knocking her plate of potato salad onto the floor.

As they carried the escapee back to her benching cage, I caught my first glimpse of an Abyssinian—a sleek, elegant mini-cougar with lofty, alert ears and a sculptured, aristocratic face. She seemed to radiate a kind of royal dignity—but you couldn't miss that mischievous twinkle in her eyes. I knew I had to have one. That was ten years ago, and since then I've learned that whoever said "you can't buy love" couldn't have owned an Abyssinian.

Acknowledgments

The author would like to thank Leslie L. C. Burchfield and her daughter Lauren, Roy and Tracey Copeland (*Cats Magazine*), James (Jim) Czajkowski, D.V.M., Arlene Evans, R.N., Grace Freedson (Director of Acquisitions, Barron's Educational Series, Inc.), CFA Breed Council Secretary Gene Rankin (Eris Abyssinian Cattery), Tom Stewart and Jim Gawronski (JT's Cattery), Tord Svenson (Juciful Cattery), and Karen Talbert (Carquinez Somali Cattery) for their help, suggestions, and guidance; Ted Brown (Tarek Abys Cattery) for the excellent color inheritance charts, and the Abyssinian Cat Club of America, in whose newsletter the charts first appeared; photographer Mark McCullough (Through The Cat's Eye Studio) for the excellent photographs; and De Potter (Nabila Cattery) and Penni Putman (24 KT Kats Cattery) for their help with the photos. The author would also like to thank Phylis Banish, Libby and Rose Basore, Sue Campbell, Rhonda Darnell, Bill Helgren, John Lehman, Robin Montgomery, Betty Roby, Nancy Sherman, Larry and Zil Snyder, and, of course, ZePunk and Bittycat for their encouragement and advice.

J. Anne Helgren
January, 1995

What Is an Abyssinian?

Origin of the Abyssinian

The cat family as it is known today began its evolution about fifty million years ago, give or take a few hundred millennia. When the dinosaurs did their vanishing act sixty-five million years ago, no land animal weighing more than 50 pounds (22.7 kg) survived the era. The mammals that survived were small, not very bright, tree-dwelling insect-eaters. These mammals now had the chance to exploit ecological niches not previously available.

As time passed, some of the early mammals evolved into herbivores, whereas others chose a diet of meat—namely their herb-eating friends and neighbors. These first carnivorous mammals were called the creodonts.

During the Eocene epoch (about fifty-four million years ago), a genus of forest-dwelling mammals developed called the miacids. The miacids evolved into subgroups that include the ancestors of the modern species of cats, bears, beavers, raccoons, weasels, hyenas, and even—dare one say it—dogs.

Compared to today's intelligent domestic felines the miacids were not terribly bright, although compared to the creodonts they were members of Mensa. However, they had smarts and ambition enough to survive and evolve into all the modern species of carnivores. The miacids survived over other developing carnivorous mammals because of their fancy dental work—they simply had better teeth than the competition.

From the mid-Eocene through the early Oligocene (forty-eight to thirty-eight million years ago), carnivorous mammals developed and diversified rapidly. The diversification produced two distinct super-families. The first was the feloidea, from which evolved the felids (cats), hyaenids (hyenas), and viverrids (civets and mongooses). The second was the canoidea, from which developed the other carnivorous families.

The dinictis, a lynx-sized animal with catlike teeth for stabbing prey, developed around that time. The dinictis was an important ancestor in the evolutionary line of the modern feline. Halfway between a civet and a cat in appearance, the dinictis's brain was smaller than today's felines'. To make up for its small brain, its teeth were bigger.

From the dinictis, feline evolution went in two different directions. In one branch were the saber-toothed cats, in which the canine teeth became even larger. The other branch, Felidae (the scientific name for the cat family), in which the canine teeth were smaller,

Female ruddy Abyssinian, Zephyr, and male ruddy Abyssinian, Sharky, owned by Abyssinian fanciers Tom Moss and Elizabeth Moore.

5

developed later—sometime between fifteen to one million years ago. The saber-toothed cats became extinct, but the felids continued to thrive. All felines, from the largest lion to the smallest domestic kitten, share common ancestors, behaviors, and instincts. Just ask that purring Abyssinian lounging on your couch, and she'll tell you she's a close relative of the tiger, lion, and leopard, so look out!

It is not known exactly when cats began associating with humans. Anthropologists speculate the alliance began in the Stone Age. Skeletons of the African wildcat (*Felis lybica*, a species originally widespread in Africa, Europe, and Western Asia, thought to be the progenitor of all domestic cats), have been found in the caves of ancient man. It is not clear, however, what the relationship between humans and felines was at that time.

The African wildcat was definitely domesticated by humans by 1600 B.C. The burial sites of the ancient Egyptians have yielded mummified remains of this species of cat. For more than two thousand years

Felis lybica, a species originally widespread in Africa, Europe and Western Asia, is thought to be the progenitor of Felis catus—the domestic cat.

Egyptians worshiped their cat companions as messengers of the gods. They honored and revered cats in life and went into mourning when they died, shaving their eyebrows as visible symbols of their grief.

No one knows for sure when and where the Abyssinian breed first developed. The best known (and most romantic) story is that today's Abyssinian is a direct descendant of the sacred cat of the ancient Egyptians. Abyssinians do look remarkably like the cats depicted in Egyptian murals and sculptures. The breed also bears a close resemblance to the African wildcat, but this does not necessarily prove the "sacred-Abyssinian-of-Egypt" story.

An Abyssinian named Zula was transported from Abyssinia (now Ethiopia) to England at the end of the Abyssinian War in 1868. Whether Zula was native to that area, however, is subject to speculation. Recent feline genetic studies have placed the forebearers of the Abyssinian breed in the coastal area of the Bay of Bengal in India.

Because there's no written evidence linking Zula with today's breed, some fanciers maintain that the original lines died out. They claim the Abyssinian was recreated by English breeders who crossed silver and brown tabbies with British ticked "Bunny" cats. Undeniably, the breed was refined by early British fanciers. Others believe that Abyssinians were imported to England in the 1800s and are a naturally occurring breed.

Two Abyssinians arrived in America from England in the early 1900s and were first exhibited in 1909. Active breeding of Abyssinians didn't begin until the 1930s, but then breeders made up for lost time. Today, the Abyssinian is the fourth most popular cat breed in the United States, and second only to the Siamese in popularity among shorthaired breeds,

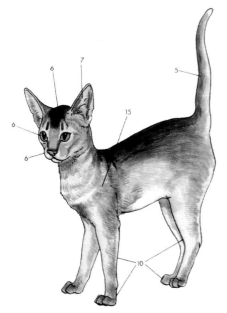

CFA Point	Score
Head (25)	
Muzzle	6
Skull	6
Ears	7
Eye Shape	6
Body (30)	
Torso	15
Legs and Feet	10
Tail	5
Coat (10)	
Texture	10
Color (35)	
Color	15
Ticking	15
Eye Color	5
Total	100

An Abyssinian is judged on two basic criteria: the condition and appearance of the cat, and how closely it resembles the ideal; however, the demeanor of the cat can also play a part. Each registry allocates a certain number of points for each feature, totaling 100 possible points. A cat achieving a total score of 100 points would be a rare cat, indeed.

according to the Cat Fanciers' Association registration totals.

The Abyssinian is one of the most captivating breeds available to today's cat fancier. With its sleek coat, expressive eyes, and lithe body, combined with a delightful personality, the Abyssinian is a perfect companion with which to share the good times of your life.

The Breed Standard

The breed standard for a purebred cat breed is a guideline that describes the characteristics that make a cat a supreme example of that breed. A perfect cat would earn a score of 100 points. A committee of judges, breeders, and fanciers draft and update the standard as necessary. Standards can vary from one cat association to another (see page 106 for the complete CFA standard). Keep in mind that the standard is an ideal. An

Abyssinian that will earn no ribbons in the show ring will still make a wonderful companion.

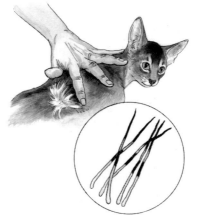

The agouti pattern is characterized by bands of alternating lighter and darker color on the hair shaft, which gives the coat its characteristic ticked appearance.

The ideal Abyssinian has a slightly rounded wedge shape head with a muzzle that's neither too sharply pointed nor square. The ears are large, pointed and set as though listening. The expressive, almond-shaped eyes are accentuated by a ring of dark on the eyelids (as though the cat is wearing black eyeliner), followed by a light-colored area. Acceptable eye colors are gold, copper, green, or hazel—the deeper the color the better.

The Abyssinian is a form of tabby, although the cat lacks the characteristic stripes (except facial markings, such as the distinctive "M" on the forehead). The Abyssinian's unique look comes from the combination of colors on each hair shaft called ticking. The lighter or ground color lies closest to the skin and the shafts of the hair are decorated with dark-colored bands contrasted with lighter-colored bands, ending in a dark tip. This is called the agouti pattern.

The American Association of Cat Enthusiasts (AACE), the American Cat Fanciers Association (ACFA), the Cat Fanciers' Association (CFA), the Cat Fanciers' Federation (CFF), and The International Cat Association (TICA), accept four Abyssinian colors for championship: ruddy, red, blue, and fawn. The American Cat Association (ACA) also accepts Abyssinians in cream and lilac, and TICA has recently accepted silver in the New Breed and Color category.

Ruddy is the most common color. The coat is a warm orange-brown ticked with dark brown or black. The red color is a warm reddish-brown with chocolate brown ticking. A blue Abyssinian is soft blue-gray ticked with deeper blue. The base hair and underside of the body, chest, and legs are a pale cream. A fawn Abyssinian is a warm pinkish-buff ticked with a deeper shade of pinkish buff, and pale oatmeal-colored underbody.

The Somali

A longhaired version of the Abyssinian, called the Somali, was discovered in the 1960s. This breed is a delightful addition to the cat fancy and is almost identical to the Abyssinian in every way, except the Somali sports a longer coat and is slightly larger than the Abyssinian. Somalis resemble foxes with their medium-long coats, large ears, and mischievous faces. They share the playful and affectionate personality of the Abyssinian.

No one knows exactly when and where the first Somali appeared. Some proponents of the breed think that the long coat was a spontaneous natural mutation in the Abyssinian gene pool. Genetic studies, however, indicate that the gene for long hair probably was introduced to the Abyssinian bloodline around the turn of the century in England. Breeders, low on breeding

Ruddy Abyssinian.

stock, used other breeds in their Abyssinian breeding programs.

In the late 1940s during the aftermath of the Second World War, Abyssinian breeders again used other breeds to bolster their bloodlines. (Abyssinian breeders were not alone. A number of European cat breeds came close to extinction in the chaos of World War II. Understandably, humans didn't have time to consider their animal companions while dodging bombs and fighting for their lives.)

Raby Chuffa of Selene, an outstanding male Abyssinian who came to the United States from Britain in 1953 and who appears on the pedigrees of many Abyssinians, is considered the father of the Somali breed on this continent. All Canadian and American Somalis can be traced to this cat.

Raby Chuffa's pedigree can be traced to Roverdale Purrkins, an English Abyssinian female whose dam, Mrs. Mews, was of unknown ancestry. A sailor gave Mrs. Mews to breeder Janet Robertson during World War II. Mrs. Mews later produced two kittens: Roverdale Purrkins, whom Robertson registered as an Abyssinian, and a black unregistered male. Robertson used Purrkins to start her Roverdale cattery. Robertson exported her cats to Europe, Canada, Australia, New Zealand, and the United States.

When longhaired kittens appeared in Abyssinian litters (which is possible whenever two Abyssinians carrying the recessive gene for long hair are bred together), the kittens were quietly given away or disposed of. No breeder wanted others to think he or she had Abyssinian lines that were tainted with un-Abyssinian genes.

Not until the 1960s did Abyssinian breeder Evelyn Mague begin seriously trying to turn these castaways into a breed of their own. At approximately the same time, breeders in Canada,

Blue Somali (longhaired Abyssinian).

Europe, Australia, and New Zealand began working with the Somali as well.

Naturally, some Abyssinian breeders wanted nothing to do with these long-haired nonconformists, and did not want to encourage the tenuous connection that the name Longhaired Abyssinian would produce. Mague, credited with developing the long-haired breed, came up with the name Somali. Somalia borders Ethiopia, formerly called Abyssinia, for which the Abyssinian was named.

In 1972, Mague founded the Somali Cat Club of America and began bringing the Somali enthusiasts together. In 1975, the International Somali Cat Club was founded. In 1978, the Somali earned championship status in CFA. Since then, the breed has steadily gained popularity and is now accepted for championship status in all the North American cat associations.

Temperament

Just as the Siamese is known for its vocal abilities and the Persian known for its serene personality, the

Abyssinian is known for its high activity level, affectionate and loving personality, intelligence, and playfulness. However, every cat is an individual with its own particular personality, likes and dislikes, moods, and opinions. Your Abyssinian may not follow the exact pattern of its breed.

However, the main reason for purchasing a purebred cat is that it is likely to follow the temperament and appearance of its ancestors. When thinking of purchasing an Abyssinian, you should take into consideration the temperament of the breed as a whole and decide whether it's the breed for you. The Abyssinian isn't for everyone—but no breed of cat is. On the cat activity level "Richter Scale," the Abyssinian is an animated ten—considered to be one of the most active purebred breeds. No cupboard is secure, no house plant is too high, no bookshelf is safe from the agile paws and inquiring mind of the Abyssinian.

Abyssinians are quite determined, and since they are highly intelligent, they "problem solve" to get something they want. If that something is behind a closed door, they'll try to figure out a way to open the door and get it. If you have fragile knickknacks, if you like keeping an immaculate household with everything in its proper place, if keeping your cats off the kitchen counter and out of your dinner plate is very important to you, a more sedate breed might be a better choice. However, *any* breed of cat will cause you *some* problems—cats are living creatures with desires and needs. The only animal that will never cause you inconvenience is the stuffed variety.

Vocally, Abyssinians rarely talk unless they're hungry and even then their voices are soft and unobtrusive (but they do purr with great enthusiasm). Abyssinians meow only as a last resort—they have other ways of making their desires known. For example, when ZePunk decides it's time for me to wake up and feed her, she crawls under the covers and, purring madly, bites my rear end. (Try to sleep through that.)

Abyssinians are extremely devoted, loyal, and loving to their humans. You couldn't ask for a better companion than an Abyssinian. They will perch on your shoulder, sleep by your side, pounce on your toes, and lavish you with "forehead kisses." (Abyssinians press their foreheads against yours in much the same way as lions do to show affection to their mates.)

Abyssinians follow you from room to room to be involved in what you're doing—open a drawer and your Abyssinian is right there to look in, and maybe help you rearrange the contents. Watch a sad movie, and your ruddy buddy will be there to comfort you and lick your tears away.

True, Abyssinians are not usually "lap cats," nor do they enjoy being picked up, cuddled, and (particularly) kissed. That's not to say they are unaffectionate or aloof; they simply relish their freedom. If you treat your Abyssinian with the love and respect it craves and deserves, you'll have a devoted, loving, and entertaining companion to share the good times of your life.

Buying an Abyssinian

Before You Buy

Owning an Abyssinian is a joy and privilege that the conscientious cat owner takes seriously. Because you're reading this book, you've proven that you are concerned about proper cat care—a very special breed indeed. But are you ready to accept the responsibilities that come with the pleasures of sharing your life with an Abyssinian?

If your prospective Abyssinian boss were interviewing you for a possible long-term position (the wages are poor but the fringe benefits are great), how would you answer the following questions?

- Are you able and willing to devote a portion of each day to feeding, grooming, and playing with me?
- Are you financially able to provide for my comfort and health, including the expense of quality cat food, visits to the veterinarian, medications, toys for my amusement, and quality supervision when you go on vacation?
- Will you provide me with the proper yearly vaccinations?
- Will you spay or neuter me?
- Are you able and willing to keep me indoors to prolong and improve the quality of my life?
- Are you willing to clean litter boxes, give medication, clean up messes, groom me, clip my toenails, and do all the things necessary to keep me healthy and happy?
- Will you patiently teach me all the things I need to know to be a well-behaved member of your family?
- Will you forgive me if I scratch the furniture, break a few of your possessions, or cough up a hairball on your carpet?
- Will you promise never to raise your hand in anger toward me?
- Are you aware that you are responsible and legally liable for my actions and are you willing to accept that responsibility?
- Will your landlord permit you to have me?
- Are the other people in the household amenable to my coming to live with you?
- Will your other animal companions get along with me?
- Will you provide supervision to the children in the household, teach them how to care for me, and see that they don't mistreat me?
- Will you still love me when I become an adult?

If you answered "yes" to the above questions, then you should be ready to be owned by an Abyssinian. Congratulations! If you answered any of the above questions with a "no,"

Two Abyssinian kittens will play together and keep each other company while their favorite humans are away from home.

you should consider if now is the right time to have an Abyssinian or any kind of cat.

Your Lifestyle

Consider your lifestyle and activity level before deciding to get an Abyssinian. If you enjoy a good frolic, if you're curious and alert, if you look at life's little challenges as adventures, then the Abyssinian will be a compatible companion. If you are sedentary, or if having everything "just so" is important, the Abyssinian's antics and occasional mischief might get on your nerves. It's wise to match the activity level of the cat to your activity level. (By activity level I don't mean whether you play racquetball or are active with the PTA. Your movements around the house determine your activity level.)

There's one exception to this rule. "Nervous energy" people who are always jumping up to do some little thing around the house may do better with a less active breed. An Abyssinian may be annoying to this type of person in that it's always underfoot.

Housing Considerations

If renting, get written permission from the landlord to have a cat before

Many Abyssinians have a fascination with running water, as JT's Moses is demonstrating.

committing to buy one. Don't try to sneak the cat into your apartment and hope that the landlord doesn't find out. Too many cats (and dogs, too) end up in shelters this way.

The landlord may have you sign a liability agreement, and may ask for an additional pet damage deposit, in case your "couch cougar" claws the drapes or urinates on the carpet. This is not unreasonable. Be sure, however, that the written agreement does not give the landlord the right to revoke cat ownership later on.

If you own a home or condominium, you may still be bound under "CC&Rs" (Covenants, Codes, and Restrictions) set by the homeowners' group or bylaws set by the condominium's trust. These rules and regulations may limit the number and kind of pets kept, and can prohibit the owning of pets. City ordinances, too, can affect the number of cats you legally can have, and certain areas may restrict commercial use of the property (i.e., using the property to maintain a cattery).

It may seem unfair to be told what you can and cannot do on your own property and in the privacy of your home. But these rules are developed to regulate those people who (unlike conscientious cat lovers like you and me) do not take proper care of, and do not accept responsibility for, their animal companions. Find out what regulations govern your complex, subdivision, and area to avoid possible difficulties.

Home Alone

If your Abyssinian will be an indoor-only cat (which I strongly recommend), consider how much of the day the cat will spend alone. Cats are social animals. They need companionship and attention. If you will be away from home all day, consider getting two cats so they can be company for each other while you're out earning the cat food.

Abyssinians tend to adapt well to other household animal companions.

If you work all day and have an active social life at night, take this into consideration before purchasing a cat. A bored, lonely cat is less destructive than a bored, lonely dog, but a cat will still find ways of expressing its displeasure. To experience fully the rich relationship you can have with your Abyssinian, you need to spend your most precious resource with it—time.

Other Pets

Abyssinians adapt well to other animals once they accept them as part of their family. Dogs and cats will become better friends if you introduce them to one another when they are young. An active Abyssinian may annoy an older, more sedate cat or dog. You may need to keep the animals apart until your Abyssinian gets to be a bit older.

Abyssinians have strong hunting instincts, so provide protection for small pets such as hamsters, rats, mice, and birds. Cover your aquarium to keep the Abyssinian from "going fishing."

If You Travel

Consider who will look after your Abyssinian while you're traveling. It's best if a trusted friend or relative can stay at your house while you're gone, so the cat can remain in a familiar environment. If that's not possible, the relative or friend might drop in a few times a day to feed and check on the cat. As a third alternative, the cat could stay at the home of the friend or relative, if you feel sure that they can keep a sharp eye out.

A licensed, bonded cat-sitting service is another option to consider. These services provide in-home feeding and care for your cat while you're away. Always ask for references and check with the Better Business Bureau to see if any complaints are on file.

Boarding services are also available, and some provide accommodations that are quite posh. Check these facilities out carefully as well. Most require current vaccination records. Indeed, you would be wise not to use a boarding service that did not require proof of vaccination for its boarders.

Liability

As the owner of a cat (or of any animal), you are responsible for its actions, as you are responsible for the

Even common household items are toys to this four month old red Abyssinian male (Copper Star of 24 KT Kats).

13

actions of your children. Laws covering liability vary from state to state. These laws usually cover personal injury and property damage. For example, if your cat bit or scratched someone, that person could sue you for medical expenses, mental anguish, and pain and suffering.

Cats can be involved in strange lawsuits as well. I once read of a lawsuit where a visitor slipped on a pile of cat vomit and fell down the stairs. (You may laugh, but the people involved weren't amused.) In another case, a cat owner whose queen was impregnated by a free-roaming tom filed a lawsuit against the tom's owner. Another good reason to neuter your cat.

Clearly, it's impossible to plan for every contingency. It's a good idea to have a liability policy that covers you against cat-related lawsuits.

Animal Protection Laws

Animal protection laws protect animals against abuse and neglect, including failure to provide medical attention when needed, and providing unsuitable environmental conditions. These laws, too, vary from state to state. Pet owners who violate these laws can be fined and/or imprisoned, and can have their pets confiscated.

Which Abyssinian Is Right for You?

At this point you're anxious to get an Abyssinian. However, a little patience, planning, and research at this stage will pay off. Remember, you are about to embark upon a relationship that may span twenty years. Many marriages don't last that long! Be sure you get the right Abyssinian.

The first consideration is whether you want to buy a kitten or an adult cat. Getting an adult Abyssinian means you will be missing the cute kitten stage. Kittenhood, however, is the shortest period of a cat's life and will

soon be over anyway. If you are not looking forward to your cat's adult years, please do not buy an Abyssinian or any kind of cat.

By buying an adult cat, you miss the most destructive stages of the cat's life. You can often obtain an adult for less than a kitten costs, unless you're buying a champion cat or a proven stud. Breeders sometimes have adult cats who have been bred and are now ready to "retire," or cats that didn't turn out to be as promising in the shows as expected.

However, by buying an adult, you will also miss the early bonding years and the joys of watching your Abyssinian grow and develop. Also, you will not know for certain that the cat received the proper training and care. Weigh these factors carefully when making your choice.

Pet, Breeder, or Show

Three categories of Abyssinians are available: pet, breeder, and show. Decide which you want to buy before contacting the breeder.

Pet-quality kittens are purebred and are fully registrable in all the cat associations. The breeder, however, believes this kitten would not be suitable for competition in the cat shows. The kitten may have too much white under its chin, or may have tabby markings on the inside of its legs, or some other minor flaw. It does not mean that the cat is not healthy or would not make a fine companion. Pet-quality kittens are the most affordable. Most breeders sell them with the agreement that the kittens be spayed or neutered when they reach the proper age.

Breeder-quality means that the cat has good potential of producing quality offspring. An Abyssinian breeder may sell breed quality cats for slightly less than show-quality cats.

Show-quality means that the breeder thinks the kitten is an outstanding example of the breed and will do well in competition. Show-quality kittens are the most expensive to buy. Some breeders separate their cats into only two categories: pet- and show-quality. Some also sell "top show;" this means the breeder thinks the cat is good enough to make finals consistently after it has granded and is good enough to compete for high regional or national awards.

If it is your intention to get an Abyssinian as a companion and you have no interest in showing, I recommend buying pet-quality. A pet-quality Abyssinian will make as good a companion as the finest grand champion, and will cost considerably less. Too, most breeders will not sell show- and top show-quality kittens to people who do not have exhibition experience.

Some people want to buy show-quality pets with the mistaken belief that the animal is in some way better or brings them greater status than a pet-quality animal, in the way they think a fancy car will impress people. Although it is normal to be proud of your "kids" and their accomplishments, the emphasis should be on obtaining a good companion, and not on what others might think. Besides, most people can't tell a pet-quality Abyssinian from the finest grand champion.

Registration

You want to buy an Abyssinian that is registrable. This simply means that one of the cat associations such as AACE, ACA, ACFA, CFA, CFF, or TICA has accepted or will accept that cat for registration on the basis of its family history or pedigree. An Abyssinian without "papers" may not be purebred—you don't know who the parents are. I recommend that you do not buy an unpapered Abyssinian. However, papers do not guarantee the quality of the cat or that the cat is healthy or free of genetic defects.

Finding an Abyssinian

Now the fun begins. You are ready to begin the process of acquiring your Abyssinian.

Male or Female

Unless you are going to be breeding your Abyssinian, it doesn't much matter whether you buy a male or female. Both make fine companions.

Price

In my area of Northern California, a pet-quality Abyssinian currently sells for $300 to $400. Price varies greatly depending on area, availability, color, gender, and show prospects. The best way to gauge the price is to call the breeders in your area.

If you find a breeder or dealer who is selling Abyssinians for much less than average, ask yourself why. Now is not a good time to try to economize. You get what you pay for. "Bargain-basement" cats may have genetic defects or have had inadequate care. Conversely, breeders who charge much more than the average may have cats with better

Sexing kittens: In the male, the space between the anus and the genital opening is greater than in the female. The female's genital opening looks like a small slit, whereas the male's sexual orifice is round.

Adult ruddy Abyssinian (right) and kittens.

bloodlines—and, then again, they may not. If the price varies greatly from the area norm, ask why.

Finding a Breeder

Unless you live way out in the country, there should be an Abyssinian breeder close by. You can find breeders by picking up copies of cat fanciers' magazines such as *Cats Magazine*, *Cat Fancy*, *I Love Cats*, *Cat World*, or the *Cat Fancier's Almanac*. All of these magazines have breeder listings. These magazines also have listings of upcoming cat shows. Attending a cat show is a great way to meet breeders and their cats. The cat associations can also provide a list of breeders for your area. (See the list of addresses and phone numbers on page 109.)

If one breeder has no kittens, he or she can probably recommend a breeder who does. In many cases you'll have to wait before picking up the kitten. Responsible breeders do not release their kittens until they are at least twelve weeks old, and some

hold onto their kittens longer. It's in your best interest that they do this. The period of a kitten's life from two to twelve weeks is crucial in its development, and it is important that the kitten spend these weeks with its mother. The breeder can also more easily judge the show potential of a kitten when it's at least twelve weeks old. If the kittens aren't ready to go, ask the breeder if you can put down a deposit to hold one.

In your initial conversation with a breeder, ask questions and expect questions in return (see list, page 18). Prepare a list of questions before calling. A responsible and caring breeder is willing to take the time to answer all your questions. Breeders may also have material to send you, including photographs of their cats.

A responsible breeder will ask you personal questions. Don't take offense; the breeder simply wants to make sure that his or her kittens are going to good homes. A breeder who questions prospective buyers cares about his or her kittens. That means the kittens have had good care and a loving environment—essential to their developing into well-socialized and healthy cats.

Meeting the Breeder

Once you have chosen a breeder, set up an appointment to meet with the breeder and visit the cattery. Sometimes visiting the cattery is not possible. The breeder may live far away from you, or may have a pregnant queen or new kittens not old enough to vaccinate. (Breeders may not allow visitors at this time, because visitors can carry in germs.)

If at all possible, visit the cattery personally. Look at the environment carefully. Are the cats and kittens allowed the run of the house? Are they kept in pens or cages, away from human contact? (The only exception to this would be the stud males, who cannot be allowed the run of the house.) It is important that humans handle the kittens during the crucial developmental stage between two and seven weeks. Is the environment clean? Does it smell strongly of urine or feces? Are the litter boxes and feeding areas clean? Are there cat toys about? Do you get the impression that the breeder views cats as companions or as a moneymaking venture?

Choosing a Kitten

When picking out a kitten, look for signs of good temperament. Look for a kitten that is friendly, alert, and curious. Tempt the kittens with a cat toy and see how they react. If a kitten cringes from your hand, or seems passive, unresponsive, or very timid, choose another. Likewise, you don't want a kitten that seems aggressive—who hisses, snarls, or struggles wildly when picked up.

Each kitten has its own personality, and some are more forward than others. If, however, all the kittens seem

unused to being handled, you may want to find another breeder.

Note: Be sure to wash your hands before and after you handle the kittens.

Picking a Healthy Kitten

A healthy kitten is alert and active. It dashes around (a little awkwardly since it's still a baby), plays with its littermates, pounces on your toes. Its eyes are bright and clear with no tearing or crust. Its nose is cool to the touch, and without surrounding mucus. The kitten's anus is clean and free of signs of diarrhea. The coat is

Blue Somali (long-haired Abyssinian). The coat of a blue Somali is warm beige, ticked with various shades of slate blue. Blue and fawn are recently accepted Somali colors.

clean, smooth, and soft and has a shiny appearance.

Look at the roots of the fur—the coat should not have tiny black particles (called "coal dust") clinging to the hair. This indicates flea infestation.

A healthy kitten should not sneeze, which could be a sign of respiratory infection. Its ears are clean and free of dark colored wax. The kitten shouldn't shake its head or scratch at its ears—that's an indication of ear mites. Gently pry open the cat's mouth. A healthy kitten's gums and mouth are pink and not inflamed, and the teeth are white.

A 12-week-old kitten should have its first and second shots (see immunization schedule on page 66) and be dewormed.

Questions to Ask Your Breeder

1. How are your kittens raised?
2. Can I see both parents, or only the mother?
3. What vaccinations have been given?
4. Has a veterinarian examined the kittens and were they found to be healthy?
5. What type of buyer's contract do you require?
6. What cat association(s) are your cats registered in?
7. Do you have references from people you've placed cats with?
8. Is it possible to visit the cattery?
9. Is this kitten pet-, breeder- or show-quality, and why did you classify it in that category?
10. How long did the kittens' forebearers live?
11. Do you guarantee the health of the kitten?
12. Are your cats tested for feline leukemia virus (FeLV)?

Questions Your Breeder May Ask You

1. Are you away from home a great deal?
2. What do you plan on feeding the kitten?
3. Will you keep the cat inside?
4. Do you plan to declaw the cat?
5. Are you planning to spay or neuter the cat?
6. Have you had cats before? What happened to them?
7. How much do you know about the Abyssinian breed?
8. Do you have a veterinarian?
9. If you couldn't keep the cat any longer, what would you do?
10. Do you have young children?

The Sales Contract

The purpose of the contract is to record the agreements made between buyer and seller in case there's any disagreement later. Contracts vary from breeder to breeder. You may find the strong wording in the contract intimidating, and might feel annoyed that the breeder doesn't trust you. Reputable breeders want their kittens to go to homes that will allow them to lead long happy, healthy lives. The contract reflects that concern. Because, as a responsible cat lover, that is your goal as well, try not to be too dismayed by the contract.

If you have any problems, concerns, or questions, talk to the breeder about them, and ask for explanations. It's a good idea to ask to see the contract before agreeing to buy.

Some breeder contracts include provisions governing issues such as declawing, allowing the cat to harbor parasites, keeping the cat indoors, and providing proper care, housing, diet, and treatment. Some contracts require the return of the cat if you can no longer keep it, and some stipulate that the cat never be sold, leased, or given to any pet shop, animal shelter, or research laboratory. If the cat is pet-quality, the contract will usually require that you alter the cat, and not use the cat for breeding.

To pick up an Abyssinian properly, put one hand under the front legs, and scoop the cat with the other hand by pushing under its rear quarters.

Support the rear legs and bring the cat up into the crook of your arm, with one hand holding the chest. Abyssinians generally do not like to be held on their backs.

Other Items

As well as the contract, the breeder will give you a few other items to take home:
- A health certificate signed by a veterinarian, stating that the kitten is in good health.
- A record of the kitten's date of birth and vaccinations dates.
- Papers permitting the kitten to be registered with the breeder's cat association.
- A copy of your kitten's pedigree. If your kitten is pet-quality, however, the breeder may hold onto the pedigree until you provide proof that you've spayed or neutered your kitten. This is a common and acceptable practice.

The breeder may also give you the following:
- Written instructions to help you with the kitten's adjustment to its new home. Other information may include details such as the kind of food and cat litter recommended.
- A "kitten kit," which may contain cat food coupons, educational materials, and information on veterinarians.
- Some of the kitten's regular food, or instructions on where you can obtain that brand of food.
- A toy, bed, or blanket that belonged to the kitten or to its mother, to make the kitten feel more at home.

Acclimation and Daily Life

Preparing for Arrival

Now that you've picked out your kitten or cat, prepare for the "mini-invasion." It's wise to make preparations well in advance of the arrival of the whirlwind Abyssinian.

Finding a Veterinarian

Before picking up the kitten or cat, choose a veterinarian, if you do not already have one. Ask other cat owners, your breeder, or humane society personnel for referrals. Your veterinarian should have experience in the care of small animals rather than livestock, be close by, and provide a 24-hour service in case of emergencies.

Ruddy Abyssinian.

Some veterinarians specialize in feline medicine. These specialists usually have the equipment and expertise necessary to give your Abyssinian excellent care. At any rate, your veterinarian should be up-to-date, supportive, compassionate to your cat, and interested in your concerns. The office should be clean and well maintained, and the staff should be knowledgeable and caring.

Schedule an appointment to take your cat for examination and testing. This is particularly important if adding to an existing cat family. You don't want to bring home a cat with a contagious disease that could be spread to your other cat companions.

Accessories and Supplies

Next, buy the accessories necessary to care for the Abyssinian. Needed supplies include a cat carrier, food and water dishes, scratching post, grooming supplies, a cat bed, a litter box, litter, and slotted scoop.

Carrier: Each of your cats will need its own carrier. Never try to put two cats in one cat carrier–even cats friendly with one another can scratch or bite out of fear.

The least expensive carriers are made of sturdy cardboard. You can buy them from your veterinarian or local pet supply store. Although these will work in a pinch, it's better to invest in heavy duty plastic carriers. These are more secure, easier to clean, and last longer. It's also easier to keep an eye on your cat through the metal cage door of this type of carrier.

If you plan to transport the cat by airplane, buy a carrier that fits under the seat, unless you don't mind your cat riding in the cargo area. (Personally, I won't transport my cats with an airline that won't allow them in the passenger section.)

Dishes: Food and water dishes can be either of plastic, ceramic, glass, or metal. Steer clear of plastic dishes, because they can contribute to feline acne. Heavy ceramic or glass that's safe for both dishwasher and microwave is a good choice. Be careful, however, not to buy ceramic dishes that have glazes that contain lead. Lead can leach into the food and water and poison your cat.

Scratching posts: A scratching post gives your Abyssinian an outlet for its natural desire to scratch. Posts

The "snuggle" type cat bed is a good choice of bedding for your Abyssinian.

can range from inexpensive to lavish. Inexpensive jobs include elongated, flat scratching pads that either lie flat on the floor or hang from a doorknob. Good, inexpensive substitutes are pieces of scrap carpeting with the jute backing side up. Cat posts, trees, condos, and pillars come in a variety of shapes, sizes, and prices, and can serve multiple purposes. Many come with perches and cubbyholes for sleeping and playing. Because Abyssinians love to get a bird's-eye view of the happenings in the house, an adjustable cat tree that extends to the ceiling is a great advantage. It will help keep your Abyssinian off the top of the drapes and the bookcases.

Whichever scratching post you choose, make sure it is easy to move. Location is important in getting your cat to use the post instead of your couch. You may want to experiment to find the right spot.

If you are mechanically inclined, you can build a suitable scratching post with a minimum of expense by using scrap carpeting, a piece of scrap plywood, at least 18 inches (46 cm) square, for the base and a 3-foot

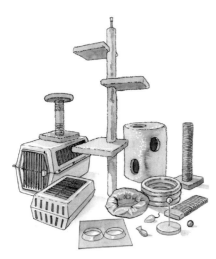

A variety of cat accessories: two types of cat carriers (standard size and an under-the-airplane-seat size), two types of cat beds (round "snuggle" basket and bean bag type), water and food dishes, cat condo, cat tree, scratching posts (single post on base, and flat-on-the-floor jute type), and an assortment of cat toys.

(91 cm) long 4 × 4 for the post. Be sure to make the base heavy and large enough so the post will not tip over when the cat is using it.

Grooming supplies: Necessary grooming supplies include a fine-toothed metal cat comb, a rubber comb, a bristle brush, and a nail clipper. Abyssinians are quite easy to groom and need limited equipment (see Grooming, page 76). If you have fleas in your area, buy a fine-toothed flea comb as well. Avoid "slicker" type brushes as they are not designed for shorthaired cats.

Cat beds: These also come in a variety of styles. When choosing a cat bed, try to get one your cat will actually use. Soft, round "snuggle" beds made of washable plush fabric are a popular choice, but you can always improvise. Beanbag chairs make great cat beds because your cat will enjoy tromping it into position. My cats' favorite bed, however, is my own. Don't be too disappointed if your Abyssinian forsakes

Covered litter boxes keep urine and litter inside the box, give the cat privacy, and help control the odor. Litter pans should be cleaned regularly to encourage your Abyssinian to practice good elimination habits.

the fancy cat bed you've bought and snuggles in beside you.

My tip: Outfit your bed with a washable comforter cover. You simply toss the cover into the washer when you wash the sheets, instead of washing the entire comforter. It makes it easier to keep your bed free of cat hair.

Litter box: Choosing a litter box is important even if your cat will be an indoor-outdoor cat. Begin with a basic pan—one without a cover and not so high that your kitten can't easily step into it. You'll also need a slotted metal or plastic scoop to clean the feces and soiled litter out of the box.

When your Abyssinian reaches adulthood, you can buy a deeper litter box, so it's harder for your cat to throw the litter out when it's burying its wastes. Another popular model has a fitted plastic dome cover to give the cat privacy, contain the litter, and help control odor.

It's not necessary to clean the litter box every day. Just scoop out the feces and the soiled litter with the slotted scoop. Don't flush the used litter down the toilet unless you get a kick out of plumbing problems. Once a week, dump out the old litter and clean the box thoroughly with warm, soapy water. Don't use harsh-smelling disinfectants because the cat may avoid the box if it doesn't like the odor.

You can use regular clay litter or the new clumping litter that hardens into an easily removable ball. It's best not to use clumping litter for kittens under 12 weeks of age.

Collars: If your Abyssinian will be an indoor-outdoor cat, you will need a cat collar and ID tags. It is important to buy a collar with an elastic "breakaway" section that will keep the cat from strangling if it gets caught. If you live in a flea infested area, the flea collar will help cut down on the number of fleas tormenting your cat. Buy a flea collar designed for cats, or one with a

A collar and lead will allow the Abyssinian a walk in the fresh air while preventing the cat from escaping. A halter style collar is best when walking your cat, but don't leave it on when your cat is unattended.

"safe for cats" on the label, because flea collars formulated for dogs contain more pesticide and can harm your cat.

Optional accessories: These include cat toys, window perches, a walking lead, and a cat flap door.

Toys: Abyssinians, of course, consider toys to be on the "necessity" list. Because the Abyssinian is such a fun-loving, spirited breed, you should provide outlets for their energy, or they'll pounce on your toes and climb the drapes.

You can find a nice selection of toys at pet supply stores and supermarkets. Avoid soft rubber toys or toys that have small decorations that your cat could chew off. These decorations can cause choking and internal problems if swallowed. Avoid toys that have long, elastic cords or strings, unless you provide constant supervision when they are used and put them away as soon as the cat finishes playing with them. Avoid toys such as balls of yarn and spools with thread—anything long and string-like—because your cat may chew and swallow them.

You don't need to spend a lot of money on cat toys. My cats' favorite toys are soft foam rubber "golf balls" (available at pet supply stores for

under $3), and a toy called The Feline Flyer, which simulates the movements and wing sounds of a bird.

Sometimes the simplest toys are best. Abyssinians make a game out of almost anything, and can spend time happily playing with a scrap of paper—if you're there with them to share the fun. Your cat's favorite game will be the one in which you take an active role.

Window perches: These shelves attach to the window sill, providing the cat with a comfortable place to watch the world outside. Buy one with a removable cover for easy washing.

Cat flap doors: If your cat will be an indoor-outdoor cat, a cat door built in to the lower part of the outside door makes it easy for the cat to come and go as it pleases. You won't have to be there to play "doorperson." Some pet doors come with magnetic strips along the sides and bottom to help keep them closed. Get one that you can lock if you go away or need to keep the cat inside.

Cat-Proofing Your House

Before your Abyssinian comes home, check your house for hazards

Abyssinians are known for their curiosity and dexterity. It's important to protect Abyssinians from household hazards.

that could harm the kitten or cat when it arrives. Seemingly innocent items can spell trouble when you add an Abyssinian to the household. Because this breed is so energetic, diligence is in order. If you wouldn't want your child to get into it, you don't want your Abyssinian to get into it, either.

Secure all dishwashers, ovens, refrigerators, freezers, and microwaves. Put away knives and other sharp objects. Cover garbage cans. Secure with childproof latches any cupboards that hold hazardous materials, such as cleaners, solvents, oils, insect sprays, and ant poisons, to keep the inquisitive Abyssinian from nosing its way into trouble. (Even rubbing up against these containers can poison your cat. Toxins that have dripped down the sides of the containers may rub off onto your cat's fur or stick to the paws. The cat then ingests the toxins during grooming.)

This ruddy male Abyssinian enjoys a "bird's eye" view from his cat tree.

Secure those cupboards holding your good china, too. Abyssinians are prodigious climbers and may happily topple a dish or two. Don't leave plastic bags lying around. Cats, like children, can suffocate themselves.

In the bathroom, keep soaps and shampoos out of reach, and secure the medicine cabinet. Cats are sensitive to some medications, and those little pills make tempting toys. After batting them a bit, your Abyssinian may try a taste. Even over-the-counter medications can be deadly. Aspirin can cause severe liver damage. One acetaminophen tablet can kill a cat.

Put any knickknacks and breakables you can't bear to live without out of reach or in display cases. Abyssinians love to explore shelving. Electrical cords should be out of reach or covered, and disconnected when not in use. Cats will sometimes chew on electrical wiring (particularly when they are young) and can be electrocuted. It's a good idea to cover unused electrical outlets with plastic plugs because cats may spray urine on them. Screen fireplaces and heaters. Supervise stove tops when they are in use.

Dryers are extreme hazards for cats. The warm, clean clothes attract cats and they may crawl in for a nap. Always keep washers and dryers closed, and be sure to look inside before you load and start the cycle. Hot irons should not be left unattended. Cats investigate objects with their noses and many a cat has severely burned its delicate nose by sniffing a hot iron. The same goes for hot glue guns, soldering irons, candles, and kerosene lamps.

Put away sewing and craft supplies when not in use. Cats have been known to swallow needles and the attached thread. If swallowed, one end of the thread can get caught around the base of the tongue while the rest passes into the stomach and intestine. This causes vomiting, diarrhea, dehydration, and depression as the intestines bunch up in an attempt to pass the string. This is known as string enteritis, and can lead to death if the string lacerates the curving walls of the intestinal tract.

Screen all windows, particularly if you live above the first floor. Balconies and open windows should be off limits. Some cats do not have good height sense and may fall.

Some houseplants are poisonous to cats. Because cats like an occasional green snack, be sure you do not have poisonous varieties (see the list on page 56). Cover the soil, as the cat may otherwise try to use it for a litter box.

Arrival of Your Abyssinian

Cats are creatures of habit. They hate change as much as humans do. They are also a very adaptable species and will make a good adjustment to their new home if given the chance.

Plan to bring your Abyssinian home when you can spend a few days there with it. Picking it up just before a weekend off, for example, would be a good choice.

When you get the Abyssinian home, let it stay in its carrier for the first hour while it gets used to the sounds and smells of its new environment. This is particularly important if there are other companion animals in the house. When it seems ready, let the Abyssinian out of the carrier and allow it to explore its new home.

Introduce it to one room at a time. Keep other family members and pets away until it has familiarized itself with the entire house. Don't allow children to pick up, bother, or scream at the new arrival. Your Abyssinian's nerves are frayed enough right now as it is.

When the Abyssinian has finished exploring, put the new cat back in its

Ruddy female Abyssinian (JT's ZePunk, owned by William and J. Anne Helgren), caught enjoying her sleepy afternoon, is intrigued by the camera.

carrier, and allow the other pets into the room. Let the animals sniff each other through the bars. This will allow them to see and smell each other while having a sense of security.

Supervise this first encounter carefully, giving equal attention to all of your pets. Because cats are territorial animals, you can expect some tension and hostility at first. Look at it from a cat's point of view—this tiny, strange-smelling intruder might be a vicious monster in disguise!

Usually the tension will disappear with time—or else it won't. Cats are individuals and will react individually; it could be love at first sight or immediate loathing. Kittens will be more quickly accepted than adult cats by your other pets. The first meeting will set the tone of their future relationship with one another. Don't leave the new cat alone with your other pets until you are sure they have declared a cease-fire.

Establish a spot for your cat's water and food dish, and a place for the litter box. The kitchen is a convenient place for food and water dishes. The litter box must be easily accessible, close by, and private enough to satisfy your cat. Don't put it so far away that the cat can't get to it in time. The bathroom is a good

It's important to teach children how to hold and care for kittens and cats.

choice; I use the empty closet in a spare room. If you already have a cat, provide an additional litter box for the new arrival.

By the time you get the Abyssinian kitten home, it should know how to use a litter box. However, a refresher lesson is in order. Ask the breeder when and where the cat was fed and where the litter box was placed to give you an idea of what the cat is used to.

Show your kitten or cat where the litter box is. Put it into the litter box and allow it to investigate. A short time after meals, place your kitten into the litter box. Your kitten should eliminate about 15 minutes after a meal.

If your Abyssinian makes a mistake, put your cat in the litter box and promptly clean up the mess, using a strong-smelling disinfectant. Don't use an ammonia-based product, which may attract the cat back to that spot. If necessary, keep the cat confined to the room where you keep the litter box until your cat gets the idea.

Never rub a cat's nose in its urine or feces. Because cats locate their litter box by scent, this will only teach your cat that this is a good spot to eliminate its wastes.

Don't let a newly arrived cat or kitten outside in the first week. It may not be able to find its way back home. In fact, I urge you to always keep your cats indoors. Many cat experts, proponents, breeders, and fanciers feel that cats should not roam outdoors unsupervised. Part of being a responsible cat owner means preventing cats from roaming about the neighborhood getting into mischief, fighting with other cats, killing songbirds, reproducing, contracting and spreading diseases, and using neighbors' gardens as litter boxes. Many people who don't like cats dislike them because their owners fail to accept proper responsibility for them.

Some people feel that keeping cats

indoors is cruel, goes against their pet's instincts, and makes them unhappy. There is no evidence of this. Cats adapt very well to indoor life. The key to insuring that cats have happy lives is to spend time with them, provide for their comfort and safety, and give them enough mental stimulation to keep them interested and alert. Even if your cat *does* miss the great outdoors, the trade-off is worth it when you consider the dangers involved. (See Environmental Hazards, page 50.)

If you must let your cat outdoors, consider teaching it to walk on a lead so you and your cat can take in some fresh air at the same time. Or you can provide it with a secured area like a screened patio or fenced enclosure, so your cat can't get out and other animals can't get in. Remember that cats are very good at climbing and jumping.

The Adjustment Period

The first week is important in establishing a good, trusting relationship with your cat. Ask the breeder to give you an item to bring home that your kitten or cat is familiar with—it can be as simple as an old towel the cat has slept on. Better yet, ask for a piece of bedding the mother cat has slept on. The scent of its mother will comfort the kitten and make the transition to its new home easier.

A kitten begins eating solid food between three to four weeks of age, and is fully weaned by eight weeks. A 12-week-old kitten has been eating solid food for a good month. Ask the breeder what food it is accustomed to. If you decide to change to a different food when you bring your kitten home, gradually switch from the old food to the new over a period of a week to prevent stomach upsets or diarrhea.

For the first week, pamper and fuss over your new Abyssinian (that doesn't mean badger and harass it).

Allow for lots of play time while it gets used to its new home. Speak softly and use smooth, slow hand movements so you won't startle it. Let the cat know you can be trusted.

Pet and play with your other pets as well. If your other pets see the new kid getting all the attention, they'll resent your new pet even more.

Abyssinians are not overly fond of being picked up and restrained. Spend time down at its level as well as bringing the cat up to yours. That's not to say Abyssinians should not be handled at all. Listen to what your Abyssinian is telling you with its body language. If it struggles, cries or looks unhappy, it's time to let it down. Too much unwelcome handling can make cats hand shy.

Teach your children how to treat and hold the new cat. Kittens' rib cages are very soft, and rough treatment can cause fractures and internal injuries. Rough handling can also cause the cat to injure the child in self-defense.

To pick up a cat, put one hand under the chest and the other under the rump. Lift the cat into the crook of your arm. Let the cat rest its paws on your shoulder or hold the cat's paws in your other hand. Always support the full body when handling your cat.

Queens pick up and carry their kittens by grasping the scruff of the neck with their mouths. You shouldn't pick up your kitten by the scruff, however, and *never* pick up an adult cat that way. Leave scruff carrying to the experts. It *is* allowable, however, to grasp the scruff to hold a cat down—particularly when restraining an angry or frightened cat.

Teaching Your Abyssinian

Contrary to popular belief, cats are not too independent or too stupid to be taught. Cats are very intelligent—they've convinced us they can't be trained.

Abyssinians are determined and

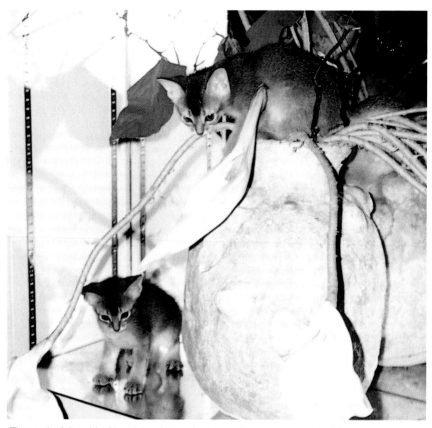

These playful, ruddy Abyssinian kittens love to make every moment of the day into an adventure.

self-assured. They know what they like and don't like. They are also very smart, and with a little help from you can become well-behaved members of your family. Abyssinians just need to know what's in it for them. Training an Abyssinian requires use of the three p's: patience, perseverance, and positive reinforcement.

No cat is born knowing how you want it to behave, and your Abyssinian is bound to make mistakes at first. Its behavior isn't defiant—it's just playful and determined.

ZePunk, my youngest, loves to play fetch, and will bring her ball for me to throw. When she brings it back, she drops it just out of reach, so I'll have to stand to get it. Requests for her to bring it closer result in a blank stare. But she always brings the ball right to my husband's feet—she's learned that he won't play this "reach for it" game. She knows I will, though. A perfect example of cat intelligence and training in reverse. Because I like this game, I've made no effort to change her behavior. She enjoys it so much.

If you reach for the ball *one time*, your Abyssinian will remember. That's why patience and consistency are very important in training. If you want to teach your cat to stay off the counter, each time you see your cat up there, you must say "No!" and set the cat (gently) onto the floor. Once your cat is down, and particularly if it jumps down by itself, praise it lavishly. Give it a treat. Praise and positive reinforcement with your Abyssinians will get you much farther than punishment. The only thing your cat will learn from punishment is to avoid you.

Teach Your Abyssinian Its Name

The first thing to teach your cat is its name and to come when called. This is easy to do. Repeat the cat's name while engaging in pleasant activities like brushing or petting. At dinnertime, call its name: "Come, Fidget!" Your cat will quickly learn to associate the words with agreeable activities, and will be more likely to respond. Don't shout the cat's name when it gets into something it shouldn't—a firm "No!" or a hand clap is better. You don't want the cat to associate its name with discipline. Of course, cats can become temporarily deaf if they don't feel like responding, even when they know their name perfectly well. But they always remember come dinnertime.

Scratching Problems

Watching your Abyssinian use your new couch as a scratching post is very frustrating. Keep in mind, however, that cats have a natural need to scratch. Rather than punish your cat, you should give the cat substitutes to scratch on and teach it to use them. When the cat begins to scratch at a forbidden spot, say "No!" and put it on its scratching post or pad. When it uses the post correctly, praise your cat lavishly. Your cat will get the idea.

Cats also scratch out of boredom. Providing your cat with toys and diversions can help eliminate the problem. Keeping your cat's nails clipped will

help, too (see page 78).

If your Abyssinian continues to scratch in inappropriate places, you can try a number of things to remedy the situation. Rub the post with catnip to make it more appealing. Make the problem areas less appealing by putting double-sided tape or aluminum foil below the area. Cats hate the feel of it under their feet. Tape inflated balloons to the problem areas—when your cat pops them with its claws, it will likely not scratch there again. (I recommend doing this only when you are home, though, so you can pick up the balloon pieces before your cat tries to eat them.)

Sometimes, you can solve the problem by moving the scratching post. For example, Bittycat, my oldest Abyssinian, had a bad habit of scratching the back of the couch. All my efforts to teach her to use her scratching post were in vain. However, when I moved her post to that corner of the couch, the problem solved itself. She continued to scratch at that spot but on the post instead of my furniture. (She just liked that spot. Go figure.)

Litter Box Problems

Contrary to popular belief, cats do not avoid their litter boxes or urinate in your shoe out of spite. Inappropriate urination or defecation means that your cat is trying to tell you something; cats naturally use elimination to communicate. It's a sign that something is wrong. A move to a new home, an addition of a new pet or person to the home, overcrowding, a change in schedule—these and other factors may be enough to cause the cat to eliminate inappropriately. For example, a friend of mine recently bought a new (and expensive) Persian rug, and immediately her cat urinated on it. The rug purchase happened to coincide with my friend's change in her work schedule. She went from a home-based business to a full-time away-from-home job. The cat associated the rug with her mom's disappearance, and by marking the most recent environmental change, was trying to send a message—for her mom to come home.

If your cat urinates outside the box, the first thing to do is schedule an appointment with the veterinarian. Urinary tract infections can cause inappropriate urination (see page 67). If the veterinarian rules out a physical problem, take a look at what's going on in the cat's life. Recognizing the environmental causes will help you to find a solution.

A common reason for litter box avoidance is the cat's natural desire for cleanliness. A dirty litter box can cause your cat to turn up its nose (so to speak), and look for a private corner to attend to business. Try changing the litter more often.

If a change in behavior occurs after switching brands of litter, try changing back to the old litter. Your cat may not like the kind of litter you're using. Some litters are highly perfumed and can be offensive to some cats; some litters just don't have the right "feel" to them. You can experiment with various litters, or try mixing several kinds. Don't mix clumping and nonclumping litters.

Location is important, too. If your cat doesn't like the location of the litter box, your cat may avoid using it. Moving the box to a quieter, more private location may solve the problem. If you place the litter box too close to the cat's food and water dishes, the cat may avoid the box. Cats don't like to eat and eliminate in the same area.

Some cats do not like to share their litter box with others. It's a good idea to provide one box for each cat. The size, shape, and depth of the box can also affect the cat's behavior. Some cats don't like using covered litter boxes. Providing a variety of sizes and types may help solve the problem.

Unaltered male and female cats spray to mark their territory (see page 36). Spaying and neutering will most likely eliminate this problem if you do it while the cat is young, before the spraying becomes a habit. If a cat continues to spray after being altered, it can mean something is bothering them.

Punishing a cat for inappropriate elimination will not solve the problem. It will only teach the cat to avoid you, and to eliminate when you're not around.

Spending Time with Your Abyssinian

The best way to keep your Abyssinian happy, healthy, and free from annoying behavior problems is to spend time with it. Abyssinians love life, and are curious and playful well into old age. They crave human interaction and companionship, and will reward you with their antics and their devotion.

Because cats are creatures of habit, it's best to set an amount of time each day to groom, care for, and play with your Abyssinian. It doesn't matter if the time is in the morning before work, an hour after you come home, or later in the evening. Your cat will learn the schedule and come to anticipate it. This benefits both you and your cat. Researchers are now discovering that people who regularly spend time with their pets have a lower incidence of high blood pressure, heart disease, and other diseases. Spending regular time with your cat will also cement the human/feline bond, and you'll come to know the joys of having a warm, trusting relationship with an Abyssinian.

Declawing

Declawing of domestic cats is highly controversial in this country. Some countries, such as Britain, have outlawed the practice altogether. Many breeders, veterinarians, cat registries, and cat associations feel that cats should not be declawed under any cir-

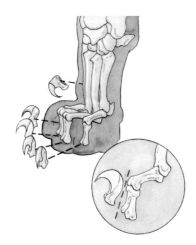

Declawing removes the terminal bone of the claw and the claw tip.

cumstances. Others think it acceptable, depending on the circumstances.

The American Veterinary Medical Association's official position on declawing is "declawing of domestic cats is justifiable *when the cat cannot be trained to refrain from using its claws destructively.*" (Italics mine.)

Before considering this surgery, you should know the following:
• Declawing is a mutilating surgery that removes the germinal cells and some or all of the terminal bone in the toe. The surgery is irreversible.
• The surgery is done under general anesthesia and the cat is subject to all the risks that surgery entails.
• Declawing removes your cat's ability to defend itself and to climb to avoid attackers.
• Declawed cats cannot be shown in cat shows.
• Some cat owners say they have noticed personality changes in their cats, including failure to use the litter box appropriately, after the surgery was performed.

Because cats can be trained to use a scratching post appropriately, make every effort to teach a cat proper scratching behavior before resorting to surgical alteration.

Spaying and Neutering

Your cat's health will benefit from early spaying or neutering. Whole (unspayed) female cats have a seven times greater risk of mammary cancer than neutered females. Spaying also eliminates problems with certain uterine infections such as endometritis and pyometra.

Neutering reduces aggressive behavior in males. Your cat will get in fewer cat fights and, since he's not driven by his sexual desires, will stay closer to home. He'll also refrain from spraying urine in your house to mark his territory.

The risks of altering your cat are small compared to the benefits, and you'll be doing a favor to the cat population by preventing surplus kittens.

Contrary to the popular myths:
• You will not make lots of money by producing purebred kittens. The costs of producing quality offspring usually far exceed the profits.
• Spaying and neutering is not expensive. It's cheap compared to feeding, raising, providing veterinary care, and finding good homes for progressive litters of kittens.
• Your cat will not grow fat and lazy if you alter it. Only too much food and not enough exercise will do that.
• Having one litter will not calm your cat down. (Have you been more relaxed since your children were born?)

The American Humane Association reports that between 5.9 and 9.9 million cats are euthanized in shelters each year. That doesn't include the number of stray cats that succumb to cars, traps, wild animals, humans, and the elements each year (no current figures are available on the numbers of these deaths).

It is vitally important that all cat owners spay and neuter their pets. Two cats and their subsequent offspring, left unaltered, can produce more than 150,000 kittens within seven years. There just aren't enough good homes for them all.

Current research shows that cats can be altered at a young age—six months for females and nine months for males. Which means you won't have to put up with the annoyance of the restlessness, the yowling, the spraying, and other signs of sexual readiness. Consult your veterinarian.

Acquiring a Second Abyssinian

If you are going to get two Abyssinians, the easiest way is to get two kittens at the same time. They will adjust better to one another, and will be playmates when you're not around. They will continue to enjoy each other's company when they grow to adulthood. If, however, you want to add a second Abyssinian kitten after your first cat is grown, follow the guidelines for introducing a new kitten (see page 25). After the adjustment period, they will usually work out their social order and at least learn to toler-

ate each other.

Introducing two adult Abyssinians to one another is more challenging, but possible. Make sure they have plenty of time to get used to each other before you put them together. I put new cats in a room with glass french doors so all the cats can see and smell each other.

It may take some time for the two cats to work out their differences, but they will usually come to some understanding with each other. If they do not, you may have to consider finding another home for the new cat.

The Older Abyssinian

With care and love, your Abyssinian should lead a long and happy life. Abyssinians can live 20 years and still be healthy and playful, although the median life span is lower.

As your Abyssinian ages, it slows down and becomes more susceptible to certain diseases, much like humans do. At first, the signs of aging are not obvious. Perhaps your cat begins to sleep more, becomes less active, and gains or loses a little weight.

The most serious problem of old age is obesity, which can lead to other health problems such as hyperthyroidism, diabetes, and heart disease. If you notice your cat developing a weight problem (you will not be able to feel the cat's ribs, and fat may hang underneath the cat's belly), it's time to see the veterinarian to prescribe a low calorie diet (see Obesity, page 48).

As with humans, older cats are more susceptible to cancers, arthritis, feline immunodeficiency virus, periodontal disease, and hearing and eyesight loss. Older cats can develop kidney and liver disease, and may have to be put on special diets to regulate these conditions. Discuss all changes in behavior with your veterinarian.

Toilet, grooming habits, and person-

Shosan's Reflections of JT's, affectionately known as Dabbers, a ruddy female who was 13 years old when this picture was taken.

32

ality changes may occur as well. Your cat may spend less time grooming, causing the coat to look greasy or unkempt. It may become less amenable to being handled, and may annoy easily. Your cat may come to react unfavorably to changes in its environment that wouldn't have bothered it in its prime. The senior cat may urinate or defecate outside the litter box due to behavioral changes, the increased urination of older age, or because of bladder or gastrointestinal problems.

You may need to comb your cat more often if it begins to neglect its grooming. When your cat begins showing signs of aging it is a good time to reinforce the cat's early toilet training, to head off problems before they begin. Extra play time with your cat's favorite toy will help the expanding waistline, and keep the cat mentally alert. You may need to change the litter box more often to accommodate the increase in urine production.

Check with the veterinarian to determine the reason for the changes. Above all, treat the senior cat with the gentleness, respect, and love it has earned by providing you with years of affection, companionship, and entertainment.

Euthanasia

Even if your cat isn't old, you may at some point have to consider euthanasia for an ailing Abyssinian. It's very hard to consider this option for a beloved pet, but you must consider your cat's quality of life over the emotional pain you'll feel over the loss. If your cat is in constant pain that cannot be relieved, if your cat is terminally ill and obviously unhappy, if your cat doesn't get at least some happiness out of each day, then it's time to let your friend go. The veterinarian will inject it with an overdose of anesthetic and the only pain it will feel is the prick of the needle. Ask the veterinarian to

let you remain with your cat if you wish. The veterinarian can also arrange the cremation or burial, or you can choose to handle the arrangements yourself.

If your veterinarian says an autopsy would benefit cat medical research, I suggest you allow him or her to do the procedure. You will have contributed to the health of felines in the future, and knowing that your cat's death benefited the welfare of felines may make the experience a little easier for you.

Allow yourself time to mourn before you consider another cat. Don't feel foolish for grieving. You've lost a loved member of your family. In many areas, there are pet grief support groups and support hot lines to help you through this difficult period. Ask your veterinarian or local humane society.

In the end, the joy cats bring to our lives far outweighs the pain of letting

Ruddy Somali. The Somali's coat is long and lush, and each ticked hair sports up to 12 bands of color. The gene for long hair is recessive, which means that the longhair gene must be present in both parents for the trait to manifest in the offspring.

33

Understanding Abyssinian Cats

Cats have known only 4,000 years of domestication and have always accepted it with reservations. Abyssinians seem to accept human authority with even more caution than do most cat breeds. They appear to prefer thinking of humans as nice companions who are so handy at opening those little cans of cat food. Perhaps it's that royal Egyptian background.

Cats communicate by using a variety of vocal, physical, and scent-marking signals, and these modes of communication are founded in species specific survival instincts. Because we don't understand "cat-chat," felines often act in ways that can seem strange or baffling to us. Because you'll be spending many years with your Abyssinian companion, it helps to understand what your buddy is trying to tell you and to understand the logical reasons behind its actions.

Territorial Behavior

Contrary to popular myth, cats are not solitary animals. They have a rich social life with their fellow felines. As cats are territorial by nature, their society is structured in a dominance controlled hierarchy governed by strict rules of conduct. The males in a feline community determine the dominance hierarchy by tests of strength. Whoever has the most muscle is top cat in town, and controls the largest area, which he defends from all encroachers. A male cat can control up to 50 acres of territory if the cat population is small.

The females are territorial as well, and their social structure is arranged along matriarchal lines with the unneutered queen possessing the most kittens on the top of the order. Although females hold less territory than the males, they defend it more fiercely than would a male with a larger area. Females are particularly aggressive if they have kittens to defend.

Both sexes mark their territory with scent and visual signals. Altered cats, both male and female, quickly lose their social status in the cat aristocracy. This is not, however, a good reason for failing to neuter or spay your cat.

Indoor Territory

Indoor cats do not lose their territorial instinct, but the boundaries in multi-cat homes are usually small—a spot on a favorite chair, or a sunny spot on the rug. These areas can also change depending on the time of day. My dominant Abyssinian lays no claim to the surface of my bed—until my bedtime. Then the bed is all hers and she'll battle any feline intruders.

The cat members of an indoor only clan will usually arrange themselves into an amiable hierarchy. The territorial boundaries will diminish with time until they share their domain peacefully, defending it from all outside intruders. (Usually this will happen. It's been ten years and I'm still waiting for that amiable hierarchy.)

Hunting and Predation

Cats are predators and have an instinct to hunt. Abyssinians have particularly keen hunting instincts and while not all of them learn to be good hunters (efficient hunting is a skill taught by the mother), they all have the desire. When faced with a fly, moth, catnip mouse, or other "big game," my Abyssinians' ears cock forward, their eyes dilate, and they get a look on their faces as if to say, "I'm gonna kill that thing!"

How Cats Hunt

When hunting, a cat will conceal itself in a place that gives it a good view of the hunting area. For example, the cat might crouch in a stand of tall grass or at the base of a wall. When it has sighted its prey, it will crouch low and hold very still. It will then stalk the prey by creeping forward very slowly and silently, pausing often to watch its intended snack, with only the tip of its tail twitching to show the cat's excitement. It prepares to pounce by tensing, transferring its weight to the toes, and treading with its back feet. Finally, it springs forward, pins the prey with its front feet, and delivers the death bite with its jaws.

Much of a cat's playful behavior serves the purpose of honing its hunting skills. If kept indoors and deprived of live prey, Abyssinians will hunt scraps of paper, the tips of their companions' tails, and even the ends of your fingers.

Bringing Home Prey

If your cat is an indoor-outdoor cat, it may bring home prey and proudly present it to you. Your Abyssinian does this because it recognizes and accepts you as a member of its family. Bringing home food for its clan is normal behavior for a cat. Rather than recoil with distaste or (worse) punish your cat for this normal behavior, your proper reaction should be to accept the gift, praise your cat lavishly, and quietly dispose of the offering as soon as possible (rodents and birds can harbor infectious diseases).

The Nocturnal Hunter

Cats habitually hunt at night. Although they can adapt to our timetable particularly if kept indoors, they still can be quite active when you're trying to sleep. Sharing the bed with one or two wide-awake Abyssinians can disturb even the deepest dreamer. Make sure your Abyssinians get plenty of attention and exercise before bedtime.

It's a myth that cats can see in the dark—no animal can see in the complete absence of light. However, cats do use the available light much more efficiently than humans. They need only one sixth of our illumination level to see clearly. When you notice a cat's eyes shining, that is because light bounces off a layer of cells called the *tapetum lucidum*. This special light-conserving mechanism lies behind the retina and allows the cat to see in near darkness.

Covering Their Tracks

You can observe another hunting-related behavior at dinnertime. When it has had its fill, your Abyssinian will scratch around its bowl as if trying to bury the leftovers. The first time I noticed this behavior in my Abyssinians, I associated it with the act of covering their stool in the litter box. I thought they were saying, "I want you to know what this icky food you've fed me smells like."

Actually, this behavior has nothing to do with feline "litterary" habits, but the reason behind the behavior is the same. Cats bury their leftovers (and their wastes) to cover their scent—to keep bigger, meaner predators or dominant members of their own species from tracking them. Your Abyssinian may indeed be unhappy with your chosen cuisine, but it usually expresses that complaint vocally.

Olfactory Signals

Humans, when compared to many species of animals, have a very under-developed sense of smell. Humans think of smells in terms of likes and dislikes, rather than as sources of information. The cat's sense of smell is nearly four times better. Cats use this highly developed sense to communi-cate and to gather information about the world around them.

When two cats meet, they exchange information in a process similar to human handshaking or ver-bal "How are you today?" type greet-ings. But rather than depend wholly on body language and vocal tone, they sniff each other on the head or under the tail. Cats have scent glands on the temples, the gape of the mouth, the chin, the root of the tail, and in the anal area. These glands give the cats an abundance of per-sonal information about each other. So when your Abyssinian stands in

Male cats mark their territory by spraying urine onto vertical surfaces. Neutering usually eliminates this behavior.

your lap and faces away from you with tail raised, your cat is giving you the chance to pay your respects. (Personally, I choose to turn down this generous offer.)

Scent Marking

Cats use scent marking in several ways. The most common form of this marking behavior is *rubbing*, and all cat owners are familiar with this behavior:

You've just come home with a big bag of groceries that you set on the floor while you secure the door against possible escapes by your active Abyssinian. Your Abyssinian is there waiting for you. She smells you and the sack you've brought in, then rubs up against your legs and against your bag of groceries.

Your Abyssinian is, of course, delighted to see you. But when she rubs against you and your sack in this manner, your Abyssinian is not saying that she adores you and that you've picked out great groceries. She means that you and your groceries belong to her.

When you come home covered with the strange smells of the outside world, your Abyssinian wants to gather information from these smells and mark you afresh as her property. You can't smell the scent from your Abyssinian's scent glands, but she can. Your Abyssinian is also spread-ing *your* scent onto her fur with this rubbing behavior. She wants to share your scent so she can easily identify you as part of her cat family.

When Abyssinians scratch their post (or your new couch), they are also scent marking. Scent glands on the underside of the paws leave your cat's personal marker on the scratched item.

Spraying

A less pleasant form of scent mark-ing (to us, anyway) is spraying. Cats

Fawn Somali. Somalis require more grooming than do Abyssinians because of the luxurious coat. But the end result is worth it.

use spraying to mark their territory. The cat backs up to a vertical surface, raises its tail, and shakes it while spraying urine onto the surface. This is another reason why cats should be altered, for even to our untutored noses their urine smells terrible. The cat is not being bad or spiteful when it does this. It is merely telling other cats (even if you don't have any) that this is its territory and they'd better stay out. Rubbing your cat's nose in the urine or punishing the cat won't do any good—that will merely teach it to avoid you.

The Flehmen Response

Cats can smell through both their nose and mouth and have a sense that is best described as a cross between taste and smell. The Jacobson's or vomeronasal organ is situated between the nose and the palate and is connected to the roof of the mouth by a duct located behind the upper incisor teeth. Cats access this sense by flehming—a slack-jawed grimace that looks like your cat has just smelled something nasty. The Flehmen response brings odors into the mouth and in contact with the vomeronasal organ. The organ gathers tiny chemical molecules from the odors, which it transmits directly to the brain. Although the purpose of this organ is not clearly understood, researchers believe that it collects sexual information.

Body Language

As with most animals (including humans), cats use body postures to communicate their intentions and emotions. Learning these signals is important, because by observing your cat's postures you can judge its moods.

A friendly, confident cat will walk with its ears forward and its tail held high with the tip curving slightly like a question mark. A submissive cat, when faced by a stronger opponent, will signal submission by making itself as small as possible—cringing with ears and whiskers flattened, tail close to the ground, protecting the vulnerable underbelly. A submissive cat will sometimes roll onto its back, exposing its tender belly to show submission and plead for mercy. A cat will also do this when it's relaxed and feeling trusting toward you.

A frightened, defensive cat will arch its back, turn its body sideways in relation to its attacker, flatten its ears, and bristle its fur to give the impression of size and ferociousness. An aggressive cat will poise low to the ground, tail swishing angrily, paw raised in readiness to strike. You should never try to pet or pick up a cat in either stance. A terrified or enraged cat might not recognize you as a friend and may injure you.

A cat's ears are especially significant in gauging its mood, and a cat's ear and head posture often precedes body stance when showing emotions. Twitching the ears back so the inner ear is facing backward indicates irritation, but could also mean that the cat is listening to sounds behind it. A cat's ears are marvelously flexible and swivel to catch sounds even when the cat is asleep.

As the level of aggression increases, the ears swivel and flatten until the back of the ears are displayed. The lower the ears, the more anger or fear the cat is feeling.

Vocal Communication

In the past, cat behaviorists have asserted that cats, as solitary animals, do not vocalize with the intention to communicate. Hogwash! Every cat lover knows there's more behind those meows than meets the ear. Unfortunately, the Webster's Cat Language Dictionary has yet to be compiled, so you must interpret the wide range of feline sounds as best you can.

Abyssinians talk only when they have something really important to say, such as "feed me, feed me, pleeease!" Even though Abyssinians are a vocally quiet breed, they indulge in a variety of meows, murmurs, and yowls that can be interpreted as greetings, demands, pleas, complaints, or challenges, depending on the tone. Toms in rut "sing" to their prospective mates, and queens make a particular "chirping" sound when calling their kittens.

Inflections and accents vary from cat to cat. As you get acquainted with your Abyssinian, you'll become familiar with its particular vocabulary and know when it wants to eat, play, and be left alone to sleep in the sun.

Purring

Purring is the most recognized of all feline sounds, and is theorized to be caused by vibrations in the vocal cords during inhalation and exhalation. Kittens begin to purr as soon as they start to nurse. The queen also purrs when the kittens are nursing, possibly to reassure and comfort the kittens, to act as a dinner bell, or just because she enjoys being nursed upon. The kittens can feel as well as hear their mother's purring. As an adult, a cat will most often purr when it is contented or pleased to see you or one of its cat friends. Abyssinians purr enthusiastically at the prospect of food.

Cats will also purr when they are ill, in labor, or dying. One of my Abyssinians purrs when I take her to the veterinarian and she's certainly not expressing contentment. Cat behaviorists now believe

Four body postures: friendly and curious (top left), submissive and uncertain (top right), frightened and defensive (bottom left), angry and aggressive (bottom right).

that cats purr in response to any strong emotion, perhaps as a way of comforting themselves.

Growling

Growling is a warning of impending aggression. Although cats will sometimes growl playfully as dogs do, you can tell by body posture whether your cat is sincerely angry or not. The sound can range from a low rumble to an open mouthed yowling growl that shows your cat feels threatened and is ready to take the offensive. Growling can develop into full-scale screams of rage or fear if the threat doesn't withdraw.

Chattering

When a cat sees a fly, a bird, a moth, or any other winged creature out the window, the cat will sometimes make a staccato, chattering sound. No one knows for sure what this sound means, although some researchers believe it to be a sound of frustration—the prey is outside and out of reach. Other researchers believe that

because cats have an instinctual aversion to flies, this sound serves as a warning. Flies can lay their eggs onto the skin of kittens and cats, and the subsequent maggots cause severe inflammation and infection. My Abyssinians take fly chasing very seriously and kill every one they can get their paws on.

Hissing

When threatened or angry, cats expel air sharply through their mouths in a distinctive sound called hissing. Spitting is similar to hissing; however, it has a sharper and more explosive sound. Researchers have suggested that cats hiss and spit as a form of protective mimicry of the snake, because even large predators balk at the sight of an angry serpent. This may or may not be true. However, when compared to the elaborate mimicry of some species (chameleons change their entire body color to match the surrounding environment), this doesn't seem too implausible.

Blue Abyssinian. The Abyssinian blue color is a genetic "dilute" of ruddy, causing the black ticking of the ruddy to become slate blue.

Nutrition and Feeding

Nutrition

Cats require a nutritious, well-balanced diet to live long, healthy lives, just like you do. Because the feline is a metabolic carnivore (the metabolism is designed to derive needed nutrients from animal protein), its nutritional requirements are different from humans and from those of other domestic animals. Cats require two to three times more protein than dogs do, and that's why dog food should not be fed to a cat. It is not high enough in protein to satisfy a cat's requirements.

The cat's digestive tract is relatively short, and therefore cats need easily digestible foods to supply them with their nutritional needs. The essential elements of a cat's diet are water, protein, fats, carbohydrates, vitamins, and minerals.

Water: Water, of course, is the most essential element. Because cats evolved from desert animals, their systems are efficient at conserving water. They can concentrate their urine to very high levels, and they also metabolize water from the nutrients they eat. Nevertheless, cats can survive only a number of days without water, although they can go several weeks without food if they must.

Water contributes to body functions such as digestion, elimination, and temperature regulation. The amount of water a cat needs varies depending on a number of factors such as the type of food it's eating, the temperature, and the activity level of the cat. Always provide a fresh supply of water.

Protein: Cats use protein to maintain all of their body systems and structures, and to provide energy. Protein should form at least 25 percent of your cat's diet, which equals about 0.1 ounce (3 g) per each pound (0.5 kg) of body weight per day. Cats must get protein from animal sources. Vegetable sources alone cannot provide the complete protein cats need to stay healthy.

If you are a vegetarian for health or moral reasons, that is admirable and I applaud you. Your cat, however, cannot survive long on such a diet. If you would have ethical concerns with feeding your cat animal protein, consider having a pet that can adapt safely to a vegetarian diet.

In order to synthesize all the body proteins a cat needs two groups of amino acids: indispensable, which are those that the cat must have but doesn't manufacture on its own, and dispensable, which the cat synthesizes in the liver. Indispensable amino acids must be provided in a cat's food in order for the cat to remain healthy. For example, deficiency of the amino acid taurine can cause heart disease and blindness in cats. Because the cat is the only mammal that cannot manufacture enough taurine on its own, it is important to choose a cat food that supplies a proper amount.

Carbohydrates: Carbohydrates are compounds provided by plants, and include starches and sugars. Although they are not a dietary necessity for cats, they do provide a back-up source of energy and add roughage to the diet. Common sources of carbohydrates in cat food are soy, corn, and rice.

Fats: You may have been taught that fat is bad for you, but it's an essential nutrient, for you and for cats. The trick is eating the right amount. Fat acts as a carrier of fat-soluble vitamins, provides an important energy source, and provides vital fatty acids that are required for membrane function, reproduction, and skin integrity. It makes your cat's food taste good, too. Fats should make up at least 15 percent of the cat's diet.

Vitamins: Vitamins are important in maintaining body functions such as the immune system, red blood cell formation, and bone metabolism. They are also essential for the functioning of the enzyme system. They are classified as either fat soluble or water soluble. Fat-soluble vitamins such as A, D, E, and K are stored in the body. Supplements are not necessary if you are feeding your cat a good brand of cat food. Overdoses of fat-soluble vitamins, particularly A and D, can be toxic to cats. Water-soluble vitamins such as B-complex must be replenished daily through food sources, because they pass quickly from the body. (Vitamin C is also water-soluble, but the cat's liver synthesizes it in adequate amounts.) A good quality cat food should provide the needed daily requirements for these vitamins.

Minerals: Your cat's food must provide needed minerals as well. Minerals are also divided into two groups. Macrominerals (calcium, phosphorus, magnesium, potassium, sodium and chloride) are required in larger amounts. Microminerals (iron, copper, iodine, zinc, manganese, and selenium) are needed in smaller amounts. All of these minerals are necessary for the functioning of the cat's body and for bone and tissue development, to maintain electrolyte and acid-base balance, and to aid in nerve cell function. The balances of minerals are delicate, however, and too much or too little can be harmful.

A good quality cat food should provide all the elements your cat needs, except water. Because nutritional needs are different at the various stages of life, adjust the food to the age range of your cat. Because your cat needs a well-balanced and comprehensive diet to provide all the elements it needs to remain healthy, you should provide a good quality cat food, and not rely wholly on meat, cans of tuna, table scraps, or snacks. Don't give your cat raw meat because of the risk of acquiring toxoplasma tissue cysts, which can lead to the disease toxoplasmosis. Raw meat can also contain parasites such as *Trichinella spiralis*, which causes the disease trichinosis.

Avoid feeding your cat only one type of food—for example, always feeding tuna only entrees, or all liver dinners. Such exclusive diets cause dietary diseases—cats need a variety of food sources in order to get complete nutrition. Variety is the spice of life, and promotes your cat's health, too.

Types of Cat Foods

There are three types of cat food: dry, semimoist, and canned. Each has advantages and disadvantages.

Dry foods consist of animal protein meals, cereals, corn and soy meal, and supplements, formed into small crunchy nuggets and coated with fat for palatability (yummy). Dry food is low in cost and convenient to store. It's easy to feed to your cat, too, since it doesn't go bad as quickly as canned or semi-moist food. The action of chewing dry food also reduces tartar buildup on your cat's teeth, and helps maintain healthy teeth and gums—it acts like a mini-toothbrush. Because Abyssinians are prone to dental disease, this is certainly a consideration (see page 71).

However, studies have shown that cats that eat dry food exclusively have a six to seven times greater risk of developing lower urinary tract disease (LUTD), a potentially life-threatening condition. This is attributed to the higher magnesium content in dry food, and also to the pH balance of the urine. When food is available for continuous snacking, the urine pH becomes alkaline, providing favorable conditions for the formation of the urinary crystals that block the urethra.

Semimoist foods have a higher moisture content than dry foods but are produced in much the same way and have the same ingredients as dry foods. They have the same advantages as dry in that they are easy to store and lower in cost than canned foods. Your cat may also find it more palatable than dry. Semimoist food will not, however, keep the teeth free of tartar.

The primary difference between dry and semimoist is that semimoist has the addition of chemical preservatives such as propylene glycol to prevent spoiling. The effects of these chemicals on felines has not been completely established, although they have been linked with oxidative damage to the red blood cells.

Canned foods: Although slightly more expensive than the other two, canned foods are highly digestible and higher in protein, and your cat may like them better than dry or semimoist, making them good choices for finicky eaters. Canned foods provide a good source of water, because moisture makes up about three quarters of the volume. This makes them a good choice for cats who need a higher intake of water, such as those with renal disease. Leftover canned food must be covered and refrigerated.

Pet Food Labels

Not all cat foods are created equal, and trying to decipher the jargon on a pet food label can give you a stomachache. Even some of the higher-priced foods are not nutritionally complete, and if fed to your cat over a long period, could result in nutritional disorders. To insure proper nutrition for your cat, it helps to know what to look for when reading the label.

In order to understand cat food labels, you need to know the terminology used. Pet food manufacturers are required to supply nutritional information to the consumer (you are the consumer, even though you won't be consuming this particular product). The rules that govern pet food labels are based on Model Pet Food Regulations set by the Association of American Feed Control Officials (AAFCO) to ensure compliance with federal and state feed regulations. The label must disclose the following:

Guaranteed analysis: The guaranteed analysis of the food lists the minimum amounts of protein and fat and the maximum amounts of fiber and moisture. The analysis may also list maximums and minimums of ash, magnesium, and taurine, among other nutrients. The word "crude" when applied to protein, fat, and fiber

By establishing a feeding area for your Abyssinian and sticking to it, you encourage the cat to develop appropriate eating habits.

Abyssinians are voracious eaters, but generally keep their trim figures. This ruddy Abyssinian looks like it's expecting a hand-out.

describes the method used to determine the percentage—it is a scientific estimate and not perfectly accurate.

The percentage of protein listed on the label means the food contains at least that amount of protein. However, that doesn't tell you how much is the animal protein that your cat requires, and how much is vegetable protein. These percentages can be misleading. To get an idea of how much animal protein is in the food, look at the ingredients list.

Ingredients list: The ingredients list must disclose all the items used in the food. The ingredients are listed in decreasing order by weight. You can get an idea of the amount of any particular item by where it appears in the order.

Statement of nutritional adequacy: This tells you whether or not the food provides complete nutrition for cats, and for what stage of life. The label will say something to the effect of: *This food provides 100% complete and balanced nutrition for all stages of*

Ruddy Somali. Ear tufts, breeches, and a full neck ruff are desirable for a Somali, because they add to the full, lush appearance of the coat.

a cat's life as substantiated by AAFCO feeding trials.

When examining this statement on your brand of cat food, note whether or not the words "complete and balanced" appear, whether the food has undergone feeding tests, and for what stage of life the food is designed. You want a food that has been test fed to cats in accordance with the procedures established by AAFCO, and guarantees complete nutrition for your cat's current stage of life (kitten, growth, adult maintenance, pregnancy, senior, or all stages). If the food label says "for

intermittent feeding only" or "use as snack," the food doesn't provide complete nutrition for any stage.

Flavor classifications: If the label reads "chicken flavor," the food is required to have only a very small amount of real chicken. It just tastes like chicken—maybe. If the label says words to the effect of "chicken supper" or "chicken meal," that food must have 10 percent chicken. If, however, it says it's "chicken cat food," it must have at least 70 percent real chicken. A cat food claiming to be 100 percent of any one type of food wouldn't provide a balanced diet for your cat, because it therefore couldn't have added supplements.

Adult "Maintenance Level" Cat Foods

A good choice for the adult Abyssinian would be a combination of canned and dry food. The cat will benefit from the protein and moisture content of the canned food while still getting the tartar controlling benefit of the dry. Buy the best quality food you can, because you get what you pay for. A complete and balanced diet today will mean fewer health problems and veterinarian bills tomorrow. Check with your veterinarian or breeder for additional dietary advice on what and how to feed your Abyssinian.

Foods for Kittens

Because they are busy growing, kittens need more protein. Their diets should be 35 to 40 percent protein, or 0.3 ounce (8.5 g) per pound (0.5 kg) of body weight. The diet should also provide approximately 17 percent fat. Choose a commercial food formulated for kittens.

Foods for Pregnant and Lactating Queens

Pregnant queens, too, require about 25 percent more protein than adult maintenance level cats. The energy needs of lactating queens is two to four times greater than for maintenance level cats. To ensure proper nutrition during pregnancy, a high protein food recommended by your veterinarian should be used.

Foods for Older Cats

Senior citizen cats are less active and have a lower rate of metabolism, and therefore their energy needs are less. The National Research Council recommends feeding senior cats 32 calories per pound of body weight per day. Senior citizen cats with a propensity for obesity should receive a reduced calorie or "light" food. Particular medical conditions such as heart, liver, or kidney dysfunction also require special diets. In determining the proper diet for your older Abyssinian, consult your veterinarian.

Feeding

Because a cat's food requirements vary depending on age, stage of life, activity level, and the kind of food fed, the amount of food will vary accordingly. Most commercial cat foods come with feeding instructions. The best guide to feeding your cat is the cat's behavior and appearance.

Abyssinians have a high metabolic rate and eat regularly. Adult and senior cats usually eat two meals a day—one meal in the morning when your Abyssinian coerces you out of bed, and one in the evening the moment you come through the door. However, some Abyssinians require a third feeding. You can then add a before bed snack so your Abyssinian will allow you to get some sleep. Kittens need to eat smaller portions more regularly—three or four meals interspersed throughout the day.

If you include dry food in the cat's diet, you can leave a bowl of this out so the cat can self-feed throughout the day. If your cat is prone to lower urinary tract disease (LUTD), however, feed the cat small amounts of dry food with its regular dinner, to reduce the risk of LUTD.

Treats

There's nothing wrong with giving an Abyssinian a little sample of your dinner or a special treat, as long as it's occasional and doesn't contribute to finicky behavior. However, unless you want your Abyssinian to dive into your plate as soon as your back is turned (or even when you're looking), don't feed the cat directly from the dinner table. This encourages your cat to think of your plate as *its* plate, and dinnertime will become less than peaceful with a hungry Abyssinian standing at your elbow trying to swipe pieces of food from your dish. It's better to put treats in the cat's bowl. Cats are creatures of habit, and by establishing a designated feeding spot, you'll have less trouble with "food fights" in the future.

ZePunk, an expert at food acquisition, has learned whenever she hears the rattle of the pill bottle in the cupboard, that she's about to get some chicken, and she comes flying into the kitchen. (The only way to get her to take her daily asthma medication, other than brute force, is to disguise it in a piece of her favorite food.) Cats are adept at learning food signals—which is why they come running to the tune of the can opener. Use this tendency to encourage good behavior. You can turn dreaded activities into pleasant activities by association. For example, you can associate getting a treat with grooming (see Grooming, page 76).

If you do give your cat a sample of your own food, be sure not to give it bones (particularly poultry bones), and go easy on eggs—no more than two a week. Never feed raw eggs, as they can contain salmonella bacteria, and can also neutralize the absorption of the vitamin biotin.

Eating Grass

Your cat will from time to time nibble on grass or graze on your houseplants. Eating grass is normal behavior for cats and researchers have documented this behavior in wild cats as well. Researchers believe cats eat grass to aid their digestion, but that has not been proven. Cats will sometimes vomit after eating grass, suggesting that grass induces vomiting to aid in ridding the stomach of unwanted

material. However, you can see cats eating grass when in no apparent distress or discomfort.

Whatever the reason, it's normal behavior, and there's no reason cats shouldn't have a nibble now and then if they want it. Some cat owners grow a pot of wheat or oat grass for their cats to eat. Purchase a grass kit at your local pet supply store. Growing a pot of edible grass also may help keep your cat out of the houseplants, some of which can be harmful or deadly to cats (see Plants, page 56).

If you take your cat for a walk, let it sample a bite of grass at the same time. Just be sure that the grass is free of pesticides or fertilizers that could be harmful.

Catnip

Catnip (*Nepeta cataria*, a member of the mint family also called catmint), is a hardy perennial herb with pale green triangular leaves that feel like soft velvet. In the summer the stalks sprout purple and white flowers that produce tiny brown seeds. It has a spicy, refreshing scent and, incidentally, has been used for a variety of medicinal purposes throughout human history.

Catnip contains a chemical known as nepetalactone, which causes the cat's reaction. The volatile chemicals are concentrated when the leaves are dried, and produce a stronger reaction than do the fresh. The effects seem to be psychotropic (mind altering), based on the behavior of cats who have taken "a nip." Catnip does not seem addicting or harmful to your cat; however, use it in moderation as your cat can become desensitized to its effects. Two or three times a month is fine. My cats like it fresh off the plant, slightly crushed to release the odor.

Typical reactions on both wild and domestic cats include rubbing up against the source of the catnip, rolling on the floor, licking and chewing, experiencing euphoria, and sleeping. The reactions can resemble the behavior of queens in heat. However, catnip is not considered a feline aphrodisiac.

Although 30 percent of all cats lack the catnip gene and couldn't care less about "nipping," the other 70 percent enjoy it in varying degrees. Some react mildly and some go wild over the plant.

Catnip is easy to grow; plant it and stand back! It has taken over most of my backyard with its growing enthusiasm. You can grow it indoors or out. However, if you grow it indoors, cut it back often—it grows to approximately 3 feet (0.9 m) high. Or you can let your cats take over the pruning duty from you.

Obesity

Although Abyssinians are not as predisposed to being overweight as some other breeds, keep an eye on your cat's weight, because obesity can contribute to a number of disorders.

Abyssinians do love their victuals. Cats become obese for the same reasons humans do: caloric intake exceeds energy expenditure—too little exercise and too much food. A bored cat will often overeat, so providing stimulation and exercise is essential.

When a cat exceeds its optimum weight for its age and sex by 15 percent, it is considered obese. (Normal weight adult Abyssinians usually range from 7 to 12 pounds (3.2–5.4 kg). Body fat increases with age, so watch your older Abyssinian for signs of obesity. Obesity reduces the life span of your pet, and robs you of precious years of companionship. Obesity also adds stress on joints, ligaments, and tendons, can aggravate arthritis, and can contribute to respiratory problems and medical conditions such as diabetes.

The signs of obesity are, fortunately, easy to spot. A normal weight Abyssinian's ribs will not show through the coat but you can easily feel them with your fingers. If the cat is over-

Four month old male blue Abyssinian (24 KT Kats Blu Magninite II), waiting for dinner to be served.

weight, the ribs will be difficult or impossible to feel. The abdomen protrudes on either side, and fat may hang down below the belly, and may appear to sway from side to side as it walks. The cat will develop bulges of fat on the rump on either side of the tail. The face will appear broader. It may sleep more and be less inclined to play.

If you suspect that your Abyssinian is obese, consult the veterinarian before beginning a weight reduction program. The veterinarian can determine how much weight your cat needs to lose and how to best accomplish the weight loss, and can make sure there aren't other factors influencing your cat's change of weight. Heart disease can cause water retention, which resembles obesity.

If your veterinarian diagnoses your cat as obese, you'll need to restrict the cat's intake of calories and increase its activity level. Although your cat won't enjoy dieting any more than you do, your cat will enjoy extra play time and new toys. Provide it with a variety of activities, such as chasing the end of a cat "fishing pole," stretching up to bat at the end of a feather, and climbing to the top of a cat tree. If your cat will walk on a leash, take it for regular walks. That's good for you, too.

A diet high in fat will contribute to obesity, so a cat food low in fat will help battle the bulge. Cats should never be put on "starvation diets," however, as this can lead to potentially life-threatening ailments, such as damage to the liver. A sensible lower-calorie diet as suggested by a veterinarian is a better, healthier choice. A healthy diet should be 20 to 30 percent below maintenance level calorie intake to produce a slow, beneficial weight loss.

Incidentally, some people think that not spaying and neutering their cats will keep them from becoming obese. This is not the case. Only too much food and too little exercise will cause an Abyssinian to become obese.

Environmental Hazards

Cats are hardy survivors and, conversely, are very delicate animals. With their curiosity and inquisitiveness, Abyssinians can get themselves into trouble, both in and outside the home. Before bringing home a new kitten or cat, prepare your home for the energetic and curious Abyssinian (see page 23).

Outdoor Hazards

Many cat experts agree that keeping cats indoors is the responsible and humane thing to do. The outside world is full of hazards and your cat will live a longer, happier, and healthier life if kept inside. Survival in the wild means living long enough to reproduce. You'll want your Abyssinian companion around for much longer than that. In addition to the emotional considerations, you have just spent a consider-able amount on a purebred Abyssinian. Do you want to lose that investment to the wheels of a car or other mishap?

Cars

Cars are the number one killer of cats—cats seem prone to making suicidal dashes in front of cars. However, cars pose other dangers besides the obvious. In search of a warm place to nap, cats will crawl up into the engine compartment of cars, where they are maimed or killed when the car starts. Engine exhaust can be deadly, too, if cats come in contact with it in an enclosed place like a garage.

Car liquids are also a hazard. Antifreeze is deadly to cats; as little as one teaspoonful can be fatal. Cats will lap up puddles of antifreeze from garage floors and driveways, perhaps mistaking it for water because it is odorless.

Rodents and Birds

Because cats are natural predators, the outside cat will occasionally catch and kill rodents and birds. Your cat can catch the parasites and diseases that prey animals harbor. Prey caught inside the house is no safer. Take prey away from your cat as soon as possible.

Parasites

Ear mites, tapeworms, and fleas are hazards to the outdoor cat and can be difficult to get rid of. Ticks pose a threat in warm, humid climates. Deer ticks, California black-legged ticks, and lone star ticks can carry Lyme disease, which they can transmit to cats and humans alike.

A run equipped with a cat door provides your Abyssinian with safe access to the great outdoors.

Prevention is far easier and more effective than trying to eliminate the parasites once they've established themselves. This is particularly true of fleas. By keeping cats inside, you can greatly reduce or eliminate the flea, tick, and tapeworm problem. (See page 69.)

Poisons

"Better living through chemistry" brings us into contact with many materials that can be hazardous to cats. Oils, paints, insecticides, pesticides, herbicides, fungicides, fertilizers, pool chemicals, and bait poisons that contain warfarin and strychnine are only a few of the items that can bring your cat grief.

Cats can be poisoned in three ways: by eating or drinking the poison directly, by getting a chemical on their fur or feet and ingesting it when grooming, or by eating prey that has been in contact with a poison. Be aware that your cat can be poisoned merely by walking across a lawn that has been freshly treated with insecticides.

Keep all chemicals that are potentially toxic tightly sealed and enclosed in a shed or cupboard. Keep cats away from areas that have been treated with chemicals.

Pools and Ponds

Drowning is fairly uncommon in cats but it can happen, particularly when a cat has access to an uncovered pool or pond. Cats have fallen into ponds while batting at fish swimming below. Cats can swim in a pinch (although it's certainly not their favorite activity), but if they can't find the stairs or the bank to climb out, they will drown.

Animals

Cats, although predators, can become prey as well. Coyotes, wild cats, dogs, eagles, bears, and other wild animals prey on domestic cats.

Cats may tangle with wildlife such as skunks and porcupines, risking injury and exposure to infectious diseases.

Encounters with other cats can also be hazardous; the resulting scratch and bite wounds can easily become infected. Because the wounds can be small and hard to see, they may escape your notice until they are acute. Other cats can also transmit a variety of deadly and debilitating diseases to your Abyssinian (see Infectious Diseases, page 58).

People

People can be the greatest hazard of all to your cat's safety. As odd as it seems to cat lovers, some people hate cats and deliberately hurt and kill them. Cats who become nuisances can be subject to retribution by neighbors. And you may have heard horror stories about cruelties perpetrated on cats (and other animals) by children and teens.

Pet theft is a rising problem in the United States, partly due to the cur-

Tattooing is a good method of identification in case your pet is lost or stolen. Make sure the tattoo is placed on the inner thigh rather than on the ear. Pet thieves have been known to cut off the section of the ear bearing the tattoo.

rent animal research laws. People called "batchers" make their living by stealing cats (and dogs) from residential streets and selling them to medical research facilities. Cats are also stolen to serve as bait in the training of guard dogs and hunting hawks.

Cats can easily fall victim to traps meant for other animals. Despite efforts to rid the country of these devices, steel jaw leg-hold traps are still used in certain areas to capture wildlife. When caught in one of these traps, the animal dies a slow and agonizing death. Cats that wander into hunting areas can also be mistaken for rabbits or other small game and wind up on the wrong end of a gun.

I can't bear the thought of my beloved kitties falling victim to these kinds of cruelties. Neither my two Abys nor my three tabbies will ever be allowed outside. They will never know the misery of parasite infestation, diseases, or fall victim to the wheels of a car. They will also never know the joy of prancing in the grass on a warm spring day or chasing a sparrow off the lawn.

JT's ZePunk thinks there might be some leftover Halloween treats in the pumpkin.

Do the benefits outweigh the costs? As a cat lover, you'll have to weigh the risks involved and decide for yourself.

Indoor Hazards

Of course, keeping your cat inside doesn't mean you've protected it from all hazards. Most accidents, as they say, happen at home, and cat catastrophes are no exception to this rule. Abyssinians are active, smart, and curious and will stop at nothing to get onto a forbidden shelf when you turn your back. Take a look around your house after you read this chapter. As your cat's protector, you need to be on the lookout for potential hazards.

Heat and Electricity

The modern conveniences that make your life easier also can make life more dangerous, to you and to your cat companions. Candles, stove tops, ovens, fireplaces, and heaters can severely burn your cat. Your cat's curiosity may get the better of it when it sees the fascinating flicker of a candle flame. Your cat's love of warmth may cause it to sleep too close to heating vents, space heaters, and fireplaces.

Don't leave candles and other flames unattended. Place the proper screens and vent protectors on heaters and fireplaces. Keep your cat out of the room where irons, hot glue guns, and welding equipment are being used.

Cats play with and chew on electrical cords, particularly when they are young. Dangling cords are impossible for your active Abyssinian to resist. If bitten through, electrical cords can burn the mouth and tongue, and deliver an electric shock that can injure or even kill your cat. Unplug all appliances when not in use. Discard or replace frayed electrical cords.

Cover unused electrical outlets with plastic outlet protectors (they fit into the outlets to prevent foreign objects from entering). This is particularly important if your cat has a problem with spraying. Because cats spray against vertical surfaces, urine can enter the electrical outlet and cause electrical fires.

Appliances and Furniture

ZePunk disappeared one day and I searched all of her usual haunts in vain. We were about to call out the National Guard when we heard a muffled but plaintive meow from the laundry room. There in the dryer, atop a load of dry clothes, was ZePunk. She had crept inside to sleep on the warm laundry, and my husband had gone by and shut the door. Fortunately, he didn't close the door tight; needless to say, this would have been a disaster if he had also turned on the dryer.

Cats will be cats, and Abyssinians will be even more so. They can turn up in the most unlikely places—including washers and dryers, dishwashers, ovens, freezers, and refrigerators. Cats are quick and can fit into surprisingly small spaces.

Keep all appliances closed when not in use, and take a good look inside before turning them on. Before starting a wash or dry cycle, it's a good idea to count noses, just to be on the safe side.

Everyone's heard the urban folktale about the woman who tried to dry her cat in the microwave (or was it her poodle?). I doubt if this really happened; nevertheless, all ovens are dangerous for your cat. Keep ovens closed when not in use.

Old-style refrigerators and freezers are deathtraps for children. Even the newer, safer models can be very dangerous for cats. Abyssinians are feline vacuum cleaners when it comes to food. As soon as they learn that edibles come out of the refrigerator, you're in trouble. Cats can suffer frostbite and can freeze, or suffocate if accidentally closed inside. You probably don't want your Abyssinian friend tromping through the jello mold, either.

Keep cupboards, closets, and drawers closed when not in use. Cats like to investigate every nook and cranny. This can turn into a frightening situation for your cat if it gets trapped inside, and dangerous if you close a heavy drawer, squashing your cat behind it.

Furniture, too, can be hazardous to your cat's health. Hide-a-beds, sleepers, rocking chairs, and recliners are particularly dangerous. Your best protection against these kinds of hazards is awareness. Know where your cat is before you fold up the hide-a-bed or lean back in your recliner.

Windows

Believe it or not, there's a term for the injuries suffered when cats fall from windows. It's called high rise syndrome. Even though cats are agile and have excellent balance, they can fall from windows when leaping at a bird or a blowing leaf, or when they fall asleep on the ledge. Install window screens, particularly if you live above the first floor, and make sure they are secure so your cat's weight won't cause them to open.

This ruddy Abyssinian likes to rest in the "cat walk" leading to the outdoor run. Notice how the window around the opening is screened to prevent escape attempts.

HOW-TO:

Protecting Your Abyssinian From Holiday/Seasonal Hazards

Gleaming tinsel, bright red holly berries, colorful lights, bright fireworks, and other items that brighten our lives during holidays can mean disaster for your furry friends. You can avoid accidents by knowing the dangers that the seasons bring to your pet and preparing for them by taking a few simple precautions.

Fourth of July

Many cats are frightened by the noise and brilliance of fireworks. Numerous cats (and dogs) are lost on the Fourth of July because they panic and try to escape the din. Cats are also injured, either accidentally or deliberately, by fireworks such as cherry bombs and firecrackers. Keep your Abyssinian safely inside and away from the noise and activities of this holiday.

To protect your Abyssinian from electrocution, unplug all electrical cords when they are not in use.

Halloween

Cats don't understand why strange people in weird costumes keep ringing the doorbell on Halloween. Many cats become stressed and frightened by all the ruckus. Cats can also fall victim to pranks and mischief on this holiday. Keep your Abyssinian safely inside and away from the noise and commotion. You should also keep a sharp eye on your pet to prevent escape attempts—it's easy to get careless and leave the door open during trick-or-treating hours.

Chocolate is toxic to cats, so keep an eye on the Halloween treats as well. If your cat gets into the tray of candy when you're not looking, a call to the veterinarian is in order. It's a good idea to stock a supply of kitty treats so Fidget won't be left out of all the fun.

Thanksgiving/Christmas/ Hanukkah/New Year's Eve

These traditional holidays are full of joy and festivities, but can be full of hazards for your curious Abyssinian, too. Provided that you take a few precautions, however, you and your cat companion can enjoy the holiday seasons.

Christmas Trees:

The Christmas tree is extremely alluring to your cat. It's like bringing a little piece of the outdoors inside, all nicely decorated with lovely cat toys, just for its amusement. The desire to investigate is irresistible. In order to prevent the tree from being tipped over by your cat's curiosity, fasten the tree at the top using heavy-duty fishing line and an eye hook secured in the ceiling. Attach a

A Christmas tree should be anchored to the wall or ceiling to prevent your Abyssinian from knocking it over. Unbreakable ornaments should be used.

large square piece of plywood to the bottom of the stand to give it more stability.

Cover the base of the tree with a tree skirt or blanket. This prevents your cat from drinking the water in the stand and perhaps swallowing the pines needles floating in the water. Avoid adding additives and tree fresheners to the tree water; these can be toxic to your cat.

String and Ribbon:

A major hazard for your cat are the many stringlike materials used both in tree decoration and in packaging. The decorations are attractive for cats; cats will often play with, chew, and sometimes swallow them. Stringlike decorations can cut through the intestinal walls, and can cause obstructions. Avoid tinsel, garland, string, and yarn, or use them only far out of your cat's reach. Attach all ribbons so your cat can't pull them off your packages.

Decorations: Buy ornaments that are made of unbreakable materials. Glass or ceramic ornaments can break and be ingested or injure cats. Because the ornaments are not being used in conjunction with an eating surface, the ceramic glazes can contain higher amounts of lead, which can be deadly to cats if swallowed. Avoid ornaments made of edibles such as popcorn or bread dough; some cats will try to eat these, ingesting the paint, shellac, hooks, and string. Instead, use unbreakable ornaments made of plastic, cloth, or wood.

You can use short pieces of ribbon to hang your ornaments. Avoid wire ornament hangers; the hooks can lodge in the mouth, tongue, and throat, cause injury to the mouth and eyes, and cause serious internal injury or blockage if swallowed.

Do not use flocking (artificial snow). If swallowed, it can cause intestinal blockage and it may be toxic. Avoid angel hair

Be sure to include your cat in your holiday activities. Extra love and attention will help reduce your Abyssinian's stress level.

Alcohol can be dangerous to an Abyssinian. Pick up and discard left-over drinks when you are finished with them.

as well; if swallowed it can also cause intestinal problems.

Electrical Cords: Lights and electrical cords are also dangerous. Cats can chew through these cords and electrocute themselves. If you choose to use electric lights, you can minimize the risk by limiting accessibility. Run the cords under a rug or blanket or cover the wires with rubber matting made for electrical cords. (Matting can be purchased at hardware stores.) When the tree is not being supervised, be sure to unplug the lights rather than turning them off.

Food and Drink: Don't give turkey, ham, or chicken bones to your cat. These kind of bones can splinter and cause serious harm. Be careful where you discard bones; Fidget can easily burrow through the trash to find them. Don't offer your cat too many tastes of the rich foods present at these times of year, either; too much people food can cause stomach upset for cats.

Keep alcohol away from cats; they have been known to drink alcoholic drinks if they are given access to them. Pick up and discard leftover drinks when you're finished.

Fire: Menorah and other seasonal candles pose a hazard to cats. Candles can singe fur and burn curious noses. They can be toppled and start fires. Keep candles and other lit decorations out of reach, and be sure to keep an eye on them.

The hearth is a favorite napping place for cats. Screen the fireplace to protect your cat from sparks and shooting embers.

Stress: The holidays can also bring stresses not present the rest of the year. Guests coming and going, new sights and smells, and the general aura of excitement can agitate your cat. Keep a close eye on your cat—all the commotion may make your cat want to make a break for the great outdoors.

A little extra love and attention will make it easier for your cat to adjust to the changes.

Premiere (alter) Featherhills Abagail of 24 KT Kats, catching a cat nap. Cats often like to sleep on appliances for the warmth they provide.

Ingestible Hazards

Cats are like infants—they will put virtually anything in their mouths. Many household items can be harmful to your cat if swallowed. Pins, bottle caps, string, buttons, audiotape, toys with easily-chewed-off decorations, and other small, loose items that can be swallowed are dangerous. Intestinal blockages mean weeks of suffering for your cat and huge veterinarian bills for you.

Discard all kitchen waste such as table scraps, bones, empty food containers, and potato peelings (particularly the eyes or shoots, which are poisonous) in a cat-proof trash can. Tobacco, caffeine, and chocolate are toxic to cats. Bones, particularly chicken and other easily fragmented bones, can splinter and pierce the esophagus and intestines, and can block the bowels. Containers that held food, particularly tin cans, can cause severe cuts to the mouth and tongue if licked.

Household products such as bleach, boric acid, disinfectants, detergents, solvents, thinners, soaps, cleaners (particularly those containing phenol), and cosmetics can poison your cat. Keep all chemicals and hazardous products out of reach. Install childproof catches on the cupboards where chemicals are stored, to keep busy paws from prying the cupboards open.

When cleaning with household chemicals, keep your cat away from the area. Rinse and dry surfaces thoroughly. If your cat walks across the freshly cleaned surface, it can pick up the chemical on the pads of its feet.

Poisonous Plants

Amaryllis	Fruit pits	Moonseed
Azalea	Golden chain	Morning glory
Belladonna	Hemlock	Mushrooms
Bird of paradise	Henbane	Nightshade
Black locust	Holly	Nutmeg
Box	Honeysuckle	Oleander
Caladium	Hydrangea	Periwinkle
Castor bean	Iris	Philodendron
Chinaberry	Ivy	Poinsettia
Daffodil	Jack-in-the-pulpit	Potato
Daphne	Jerusalem cherry	Rhododendron
Datura	Jimsonweed	Rhubarb
Dieffenbachia	Larkspur	Skunk cabbage
Elephants ear	Lily of the valley	Tulip
Euonymus	Mistletoe	Wisteria
Foxglove	Monkshood	Yew

Symptoms of Trouble

Symptoms	Probable Cause
Choking, gagging, salivating, difficulty breathing, abdominal pain	Swallowed objects
Unconsciousness, shock, cyanosis, breathing difficulty, circulatory collapse, burns in the mouth	Electrocution
Redness of skin, blisters, swelling, shock	Burns
Mouth irritation, drooling, vomiting, diarrhea, abdominal pain, seizures, coma	Poisoning

Your cat will then lick the chemical off its paws during grooming.

Medications that are innocuous to humans can be deadly to cats. Even vitamins in human doses can be deadly to cats. Fortunately, this kind of poisoning is easy to prevent. Don't take pills out of their bottles and leave them unattended on the table or counter, even for a second. Leave them in their containers until you're ready to take them, and be sure you replace the lids tightly when you're through. Abyssinians, with their unfailing nose for mischief, could knock them over and spill the contents. Keep all medications out of reach when not in use, and discard all old medication. Never give medication intended for humans to your cat unless your veterinarian has advised you to do so.

Plants

Houseplants are a significant area of concern, because cats will often indulge their craving for greenery by grazing on your indoor foliage. Some plants are harmless to your cat. Others can kill.

Fortunately, plant poisoning is fairly rare in cats. Refer to the list of poisonous plants on page 56 before you buy plants for your home. This is a list of common plants and is by no means complete. Many other plants are toxic.

Many of these plants also can be found outdoors and can be hazardous to outdoor cats. By keeping your Abyssinian indoors you can eliminate this danger.

Abyssinians love to get into the Christmas spirit, as ZePunk is demonstrating.

57

Health Care and Diseases

Entire books have been written about the diseases and disorders of felines. This section touches upon the most common and critical of the infectious diseases, and the most common ailments and conditions. However, if your cat's behavior changes or if it develops a persistent symptom, don't self-diagnose. Take your cat to the veterinarian for a diagnosis and determination of the proper treatment. Cats are good at concealing their illnesses until they are very sick, and time may be of the essence when you finally notice something is wrong.

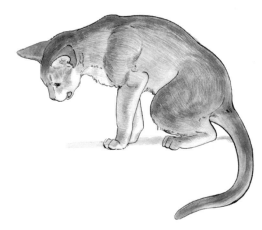

Abdominal pain will cause a cat to crouch in a "tucked up" posture.

Infectious Diseases

Feline Panleukopenia Virus (FPV, Feline Distemper)

In unvaccinated cat populations, panleukopenia is one of the most contagious and destructive feline diseases. Although cats of any age can get this virus, it is most virulent in kittens, because the virus replicates only in host cells that are actively reproducing. The virus is transmitted by direct contact with an infected cat's feces, urine, saliva, fleas, or vomitus. The virus can also be contracted indirectly from contact with contaminated objects, such as food bowls, litter pans, and bedding. Humans can also spread this virus. You can bring the virus home if you pet an infected cat or hold it on your lap, or step in the excrement, urine, or blood fluid of an infected cat.

The onset of this disease is sudden and is characterized by any or all of these symptoms: fever, loss of appetite, dehydration, depression, coat dullness, vomiting, and painful abdomen. A common laboratory finding is a drop in the cat's white blood cell count. Infected, urine, or blood cats often assume a hunched position.

The mortality rate for this disease is high. The best defense is vaccination (see vaccination chart, page 66).

Feline Leukemia Virus (FeLV)

Feline leukemia virus (FeLV), a virus of the family of Retroviridae, kills more cats than any other feline

HOW-TO:
Brushing Your Cat's Teeth

Cats get cavities just like people do. But unlike humans, cats develop tooth decay just under the gum line. This can cause gingivitis as well. Because of the location, it's difficult to see these cavities until they are well advanced and threatening the entire tooth. To prevent tooth loss, it's important to brush your cat's teeth regularly and to provide periodic dental checkups with your veterinarian.

Dental Products

There are a number of products on the market to help keep your Abyssinian's smile bright. Stannous flouride products like QyGel™ are used to prevent dental disease by strengthening the enamel, inhibiting plaque formation, and acting as an antimicrobial agent. Products such as CHX™ Chlorhexidine gel are used to promote oral hygiene by providing an antibacterial agent to reduce inflammation of the gums. Your veterinarian can prescribe both products.

You can also buy cat dentifrices (toothpastes) to use for daily brushing to remove food particles and prevent the buildup of plaque and tartar. Use a toothpaste designed for cats such as C.E.T.®, available at many veterinarians' offices and pet supply stores. You can also dilute hydrogen peroxide to clean the teeth and gums. Don't use human toothpaste as the foaming is frightening to cats

and the swallowed paste may cause stomach upset.

I know it's an inconvenience, but you must brush your Abyssinian's teeth regularly (twice or three times a week) and resign yourself to the expense of having your cat's teeth cleaned approximately once a year. Because having a cat's teeth cleaned professionally requires the use of anesthetic that can be dangerous for your cat, keep the teeth brushed so your cat can go at least a year between cleanings. Fortunately, brushing your cat's teeth isn't as difficult as it sounds; it just takes patience and gentleness.

You can use a soft rag to clean your cat's teeth or a tooth brush purchased at a pet supply store. If you choose to use a toothbrush designed for humans, buy the smallest size available (a child's size is good) with the gentlest bristles possible. It's better to get a tooth brush designed for cats. I use a soft rubber brush formed like the tip of a glove so it slips over my finger. It gives me better control and reduces the risk of accidentally hurting my cats while cleaning their teeth. It's best to have one brush for each cat to prevent the transmission of bacteria.

The instructions on the package of cat toothpaste I use include advice on how to acquaint your cat with toothbrushing. The label gushes that soon you and your cat will begin to look forward to this precious time together. However, none of my cats have ever learned to enjoy having their teeth brushed. Yours probably won't, either.

You *can* get your cat to tolerate the process without too

much trouble if you exercise patience and if you brush your cat's teeth regularly. It's very important not to hurt your cat, because that will make your cat dread the process and hide under the bed as soon as you bring out the toothpaste. When you begin, limit the time to a few seconds and talk encouragingly to your cat the entire time.

Gently brush the tooth in a circular motion, being very gentle on the sensitive gums. Talk soothingly to your cat and when you're finished, praise it warmly and give it a treat. Soon your Abyssinian will learn this is just another of those strange things humans insist on doing and learn to accept it with resignation, if not enthusiasm.

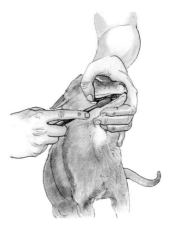

It is easier to brush your cat's teeth with a helper, however you can do it alone. Hold the cat's head from the top, with your palm covering the top of the head and your thumb and index finger holding the corners of the mouth. Gently push back one corner of the mouth and insert the tooth brush between the teeth and the cheek. It is usually not necessary to brush the inside of the teeth.

Ruddy Abyssinian (left) and red Abyssinian (right). Healthy Abyssinians have bright, clear eyes, clean teeth, and shiny coats.

disease, and is second only to the automobile in numbers of deaths. FeLV kills by blocking a cat's natural ability to fight germs, so death occurs from secondary ailments such as pneumonia, infections, and stomach problems.

Common modes of transmission are via saliva, particularly through activities such as mutual grooming, eating from the same bowl, or biting wounds. It can also be transmitted via feces and urine; sharing a litter box with an infected cat can lead to infection. The disease can also be transmitted via the respiratory secretions produced when an infected cat sneezes. However, FeLV does not live long outside the body, and household cleaners kill the virus almost immediately. The risk of infecting your cat by petting a strange cat is small, although washing your hands after handling an unfamiliar animal is always a good practice.

A significant number of the cats exposed to FeLV become immune to it. These cats are usually healthy and stress-free. Some cats can go months or years carrying the dormant virus, appearing completely healthy, until stress, diet, or other factors cause the virus to activate. If the cat's immune system does not fight off the virus, the disease eventually spreads to the bone marrow and contaminates the blood cells. The blood cells then transport the disease to other parts of the body.

When the virus enters the blood cell, it enters the nucleus and "hijacks" the cell, forcing it to produce either more of the virus, or to produce cancer cells. Because this process does

Blue Abyssinian kitten. Notice the impressive ears on this youngster.

not destroy the producer cells, the virus has a much faster replication rate than other viruses.

FeLV attacks the body three ways: by causing tumors that eventually interrupt the body's normal functions, by attacking the growing blood cells in the bone marrow, causing anemia and slower clotting, and by suppressing the immune system so the cat cannot fight off infections.

The symptoms of the disease vary, because the cat usually dies of the secondary causes. One of the chief symptoms of the onset of the acute phase is marked, rapid weight loss. Also watch for symptoms such as sluggishness, poor appetite, and recurring colds and infections. Once the symptoms appear, the cat usually dies within three months to three years. There is no cure.

The only remedy for this killer is prevention. Fighting FeLV involves three important steps: testing, vaccinating, and isolating infected cats. It's necessary to test for FeLV before vaccination because vaccinating an already infected cat is useless and will give you a false sense of security. An infected cat that has been vaccinated will continue to spread the disease. It is essential to vaccinate indoor-outdoor cats, or cats that will have contact with other felines.

FeLV was once thought to be a zoonotic disease—that it could pass from cats to humans. However, there is no evidence that any human illness has ever been caused by FeLV.

Feline Immune Deficiency Virus (FIV)

Feline immune deficiency virus (FIV) is a newly recognized feline virus belonging to the Retrovirus family. Although related to FeLV and other retroviruses, FIV does not cause cancer like FeLV does. Rather, FIV is in the lentivirus subgroup, as is infectious anemia in horses and acquired immunodeficiency syndrome (AIDS) in humans. (You *cannot* get AIDS from an FIV-positive cat.)

Researchers have found that the common mode of transmission is bite wounds—saliva transports the virus. Mothers can also transmit FIV to kittens during gestation. Like human AIDS, casual contact among cats is not an efficient means of transmission. Unlike the human AIDS virus, however, sexual contact is not the primary means of spreading FIV.

When the disease enters the body, the virus travels to the lymph nodes, where it replicates in specific white blood cells known as T-cells. This causes enlargement of the lymph nodes, which usually is not noticed by the cat owner. Over the next days, weeks, or months, the cat may develop a fever and the white blood cell count drops. The cat may also develop anemia at this point, but may appear completely healthy for months or even years after infection. Eventually, the signs of the disease begin to appear as the disease breaks down the immune system, allowing secondary infections to take hold.

Because the symptoms of the secondary infections vary, FIV is hard to identify and is easily confused with FeLV. The symptoms can include general malaise, loss of appetite, pain during eating caused by gingivitis, weight loss, fever (103°F [39.4°] or higher), diarrhea, reproductive problems, seizures and other neurologic disorders, and chronic or recurrent infections of the skin, bladder, and upper respiratory tract.

The treatment options are limited to treating the secondary infections with antibiotics and antifungal drugs and the use of anti-inflammatory drugs to control the gingivitis. Steroids may help combat the weight loss. Supportive care, including diet, blood transfusions, and intravenous fluids, are often necessary.

No cure and no vaccines are currently available for FIV. The best way to keep a cat from getting this virus is to keep it away from other cats. By keeping cats inside, and testing any new cat brought into the household, you can prevent your cat from contracting the disease.

Although the disease is similar to human AIDS, FIV is species specific. *It does not cause human AIDS and poses no threat to humans or nonfeline companion animals.*

Feline Infectious Peritonitis (FIP)

The feline infectious peritonitis (FIP) virus belongs to a group of viruses called coronaviruses, so named because of the spikelike projections on the virus that resemble the sun's corona. The FIP virus infects white blood cells called macrophages and circulating monocytes. These cells are part of the immune system designed to destroy viruses; ironically, these cells help transport the virus throughout the body. In the tissues where the virus takes hold, an inflammatory reaction takes place caused by the immune system and the antibodies created to fight the disease. The interaction of the virus and the immune system causes the damage to the tissues. Although the disease was named after the inflammatory reaction on the peritoneum, or the lining of the abdomen, the disease causes other types of lesions in other parts of the body as well.

There are two types of FIP. The "wet" form of the disease is characterized by the accumulation of fluid within a cat's abdomen or chest, which results in laborious breathing. Other symptoms include fever, listlessness, loss of appetite, and weight loss. Usually the cat will live only a few days or weeks after the initial signs appear.

The "dry" form of the disease progresses more slowly and the symptoms are more ambiguous. The symptoms vary, depending on the body areas affected, but usually include lethargy, weight loss, and intermittent fever that does not respond to antibiotics. The cat may also show signs of liver or kidney failure. A cat with the dry form of FIP will usually die within weeks or months of getting the disease.

The route of transmission of this virus is not completely understood. Researchers think it is passed by cat-to-cat contact, and may be contracted by contact with contaminated objects such as feeding dishes and litter boxes. Unlike the panleukopenia virus, which is highly resistant, the FIP virus can be killed by most household disinfectants.

Although there have been a few reported cases of FIP going into remission, the disease is usually fatal; there is no known effective treatment or cure. The usual approach is supportive care, immune-suppressing medications, and antibiotics.

Fortunately, there is an effective and safe intranasal vaccine for FIP. All cats that will have contact with other cats should receive vaccination.

Feline Viral Rhinotracheitis (FVR)

Feline viral rhinotracheitis, also called FVR, rhino, and feline herpes, is an acute disease that affects the respiratory system and is caused by the feline herpes virus. The symptoms are similar to the common cold, and include sneezing and coughing in the initial stages. Next the eyes become red, swollen, and sensitive to light. The eyes produce a watery discharge, and the nose usually runs and forms a crust. A fever may also be present, and the cat may seem depressed and may stop eating.

The disease may last several days or may linger for several weeks depending on the severity of exposure and the virulence of the virus. Like the cold virus, FVR transmits easily from one cat to another through direct contact, shared feeding and water dishes, and litter pans, or by aerosol droplets drifting in the air from the emissions of an infected cat. FVR can also be carried on the hands, clothes, or feet of humans caring for infected cats.

Treatment for FVR is usually symptomatic. Antibiotics are given to treat secondary bacterial infections. In severe cases, fluids are given to overcome dehydration. Oxygen is given if lack of respiratory function decreases the cat's oxygen intake. As with the common cold, a "tincture of time" is the only cure.

Feline Calicivirus (FCV)

Feline calicivirus (FCV) is a respiratory disease similar to FVR, but the infection is usually milder. However, of all the respiratory diseases, FCV is the most likely to cause pneumonia, which can be fatal, particularly to young kittens. Treatment is the same as for FVR.

FVR, FCV, and other cat respiratory diseases such as feline chlamydiosis are common and easily spread, particularly in catteries. One major reason for the ease of spread is that even after the cat has recovered from the disease and is no longer symptomatic, the animal carries the disease and can transmit it to other cats. FVR is intermittently shed from the back of the mouth for many months after the cat has recovered. Cats infected with calicivirus shed the virus from the throat and sometimes the feces for a long time after recovery. In order to insure that your cat is protected against respiratory diseases, keep the proper vaccinations current and prevent exposure to infected cats.

Rabies

Rabies (also called hydrophobia) is one of the best-known and most feared of diseases. Once the clinical signs manifest, the mortality rate is virtually 100 percent. This disease can infect humans as well as cats, dogs, bats, skunks, foxes, raccoons, and other warm-blooded animals. Once the virus enters the body, it moves from the muscle tissue at the point of entry to the nerve endings. It moves up the nerve pathways until it reaches the spinal cord and the brain.

The rabies virus is secreted in vast numbers in the infected animal's saliva, which makes the bite of an infected animal the primary means of transmission. Because many infected animals go through a furious phase in which they become highly aggressive and will try to bite other animals and humans, rabid animals are very dangerous. (Why the disease causes this behavior is unknown. Humans

infected with the disease go through a furious phase as well.)

The furious phase may last from one to seven days. During this time the animal may at first become withdrawn and hide in dark places. In a few days, it becomes irritable and will attack anyone within reach. Infected animals also seem deranged and will lunge at and try to bite imaginary objects. Cats are very dangerous when in the furious phase because they're extremely quick and will attack viciously.

The disease then shifts to the paralytic or dumb phase, the final phase before death. The head and neck muscles become paralyzed, making it difficult for the animal to swallow (hence the name hydrophobia, because this symptom was mistaken for a fear of water). Complete paralysis soon follows, then death.

Even if your cat will be always indoors, keep the cat's rabies vaccination current. This disease is just too dangerous to take a chance.

Vaccinations

The good news is that you can prevent some of the most common and dangerous diseases with proper vaccinations. Although no vaccination is 100 percent effective, vaccinations have saved countless feline lives, and should be a basic part of your cat's health care.

Vaccinations are particularly important if your cat will be outside, even for short periods and under supervision. Cats can be quickly exposed to the transmitters of diseases—other cats and their wastes, parasites, and wildlife. You should, however, have the yearly vaccinations done whether you intend to let the cat outside or not. Someone might leave the door or window open. Some states require certain vaccinations, such as rabies. A cat can be confiscated if it bites someone

Blue Abyssinian. Blue Abyssinians were noticed in Abyssinian litters as far back as the 1950s, but were not accepted for CFA championship until 1984.

and you cannot prove that it has been vaccinated. The cost is minimal compared to your cat's life and your peace of mind.

Vaccinations work by introducing a modified form of the disease into the cat's system, causing the cat's body to develop antibodies against the disease organisms. This usually results in immunity.

There are several types of vaccines available. Inactivated vaccines (also called killed-virus vaccines) have been treated so the infectious agent cannot infect the cat. These vaccines are very safe, but require longer to produce the desired immune response.

Attenuated vaccines (also called modified live-virus vaccines or MLV), contain live viruses that have been altered so they don't produce the clinical disease. These vaccines create a rapid immune response. However, in some cases and for a short period, MLV vaccines can infect unprotected cats who come in contact with immunized cats.

In the third type of vaccine, subunit vaccine, part of the infectious agent is separated from the rest and used to stimulate the immune system into creating antibodies against the whole disease. These vaccines are also quite safe.

A fourth type of vaccine that will doubtless become widely used in the future is genetically recombinant vaccines, such as a type of vaccine that is now becoming available for feline leukemia. The vaccine was engineered to produce the specific protein that allows the virus to attach to the cell. This protein stimulates the immune system to respond with immunity. What was once science fiction is being used in practical application today.

Although vaccines are usually safe and adverse effects are rare, occasionally life-threatening systemic reactions can occur. Because of the possible complications, only qualified veterinary personnel should give vaccinations. Consult the vaccination chart below for the vaccination intervals.

Illnesses and Disorders

Abyssinians are a bit more susceptible to some conditions and illnesses

Recommended Vaccinations

Disease	Type Vaccination	1st Vaccination	2nd Vaccination	Revaccination
Panleukopenia	Inactivated, MLV, MLV-IN	8–10 weeks	12–14 weeks	yearly
Calicivirus	Inactivated, MLV, MLV-IN	8–10 weeks	12–14 weeks	yearly
Rhinotracheitis	Inactivated, MLV, MLV-IN	8–10 weeks	12–14 weeks	yearly
Rabies	Inactivated	12 weeks	64 weeks	triannually
Leukemia	Inactivated	9 weeks	12 weeks	yearly
Chlamydiosis	Live-attenuated	8–10 weeks	12–14 weeks	yearly

than other breeds, particularly to gingivitis and certain kidney dysfunctions. Be familiar with these and the following ailments and their symptoms so your cat can receive prompt and proper treatment.

Hair Balls

Hair balls are dense balls of swallowed hair that accumulate in the stomach. Even shorthaired breeds like the Abyssinian are susceptible. Cats groom themselves regularly, and because they have raspy, rough tongues that are perfect for collecting hair, cats swallow bits of hair in the process. Usually the hair moves through the digestive tract and passes out with the feces. Sometimes, however, the hair accumulates in the stomach, forming compact balls, and these must be expelled. Usually the cat vomits them up on the rug. This is not a great cause for concern (except for your rug), as long as it's occasional.

These balls, however, can also pass through the digestive tract and lead to obstructions. Symptoms include frequent vomiting, loss of appetite, wheezing, retching, and in some cases a swollen and painful abdomen. If your cat displays any of the above symptoms, take it to your veterinarian immediately. Sometimes surgery is necessary.

To help your cat deal with the swallowed hair, regular grooming and preventive measures such as the administration of petrolatum products like Kittymalt or Petromalt will curb much of the problem. Use as directed—too much can hinder the absorption of fat-soluble vitamins. For stubborn or persistent cases, a high-fiber diet will help your cat pass the hair through its system more easily.

Lower Urinary Tract Disease (LUTD)

Anyone who's had a urinary tract infection can attest to the discomfort it causes. It's no different for your feline friends, and this disease can be life-threatening if a blockage occurs. Formerly called FUS, lower urinary tract disease (LUTD) is a term for a group of disorders and diseases that affect the urinary tract and can be caused by a variety of factors including bacteria, fungus, parasites, anatomic abnormalities, and tumors. The symptoms of LUTD include inappropriate urination such as dribbling urine in unusual spots, frequent voiding of small quantities of urine, straining at the end of urination, and blood in the urine. The cat may also exhibit listlessness, poor appetite, and excessive thirst.

Cats with LUTD develop sand size crystals in their urine, which, combined with mucus and sloughed tissue and blood, can form blockages in the urinary tract. Too much magnesium and phosphorus in a cat's diet can contribute to the forming of these crystals.

These blockages occur more frequently in male cats than in females. If your cat strains to urinate and produces only a tiny amount of urine, take your cat to the veterinarian immediately. This is a life-threatening emergency.

Treatment of LUTD includes special diets that control the magnesium and phosphorus levels of the food as well as the pH level, which is also a contributing factor in the formation of crystals.

Eye Ailments

Conjunctivitis, inflammation of the membrane that lines the eyelids and protects the eyeball, is quite common in cats. It can be caused by several factors, including allergens and irritants from the environment such as bacteria, viruses, plant pollens, and cigarette smoke. Symptoms include discharge from the eye (particularly discharge that is cloudy or discolored), blinking, exposed third eyelid, and swelling and

This outdoor run allows JT's Abyssinians safe access to the fresh air and sunshine. Cats should be vaccinated before they are allowed outside.

redness of the third eyelid. If you notice that your cat's third eyelid (also called the haw or nictating membrane) peeks out from the inner corner of your cat's eyes and doesn't retreat back under the eyelid as it normally does, it's time to see the veterinarian.

Conjunctivitis is usually not serious unless caused by bacteria or accompanied with diseases such as upper respiratory infection, rhinotracheitis, or calicivirus. If you notice any of the above symptoms, see your veterinarian to be sure it's not something serious. Even minor conjunctivitis cannot be ignored; see your veterinarian as soon as possible.

Blinking, redness, and watery eyes and irritation are also signs that your cat's eye may have been injured. The most common eye injury is the dam-

age resulting from the claws of another cat. As this can result in a serious infection, see your veterinarian promptly. Your veterinarian can diagnose the cause and prescribe ointments that will help the eye heal.

Ear Problems

If you notice dark brown, waxy discharge from the ears, or if your cat shakes its head or scratches at its ears, it's usually a sign that your cat has an ear infection caused by bacteria or fungi, a parasitic infestation, or a foreign body it has picked up, such as a foxtail. Your cat needs to see the veterinarian for any of these conditions.

The parasite that infests the ears is the ear mite, which is a tiny creature that lives inside the ear canal and sucks blood from the wall of the ear. If not treated, ear mites and infections can cause permanent, disfiguring damage to the ears, and in some cases, can even kill your cat. Mites pass easily from one cat to another and from mother to kittens. Fortunately, your veterinarian can easily treat mite infestation.

Foxtails, the seed pods from a grass plant, can lodge in the ears (and eyes, nose, and fur) and work their way into the brain, killing your cat. Foxtails must be removed by your veterinarian immediately.

Kidney Disorders

The Abyssinian breed is prone to the renal disease amyloidosis. This disease occurs when an insoluble protein called amyloid is deposited in the kidneys, causing lesions, dysfunction, and eventual kidney failure. The cause is unknown. Abyssinians usually do not respond to treatment, and kidney failure results as medullary fibrosis and tubular damage increase. Why Abyssinians are prone to this disease is not known, except that the disease is thought to be passed genetically from generation to generation.

The progression of the disease can be quick or slow; some Abyssinians can live up to ten years or more. Unfortunately, most Abyssinians with the disease die before they reach five years old. The disease is considered incurable except by "heroics" such as kidney transplants, which are now being performed at some universities. Special diets low in protein and high in fat content can sometimes slow the progression of the disease. This type of diet doesn't work the kidneys as hard as the standard high-protein cat diet.

The symptoms of the disease are chronic weight loss, rough or dull coat, dehydration, and gingivitis. A diagnosis of amyloidosis can be confirmed by a biopsy of the kidney. Initial tests to rule out other types of kidney dysfunction include urine and blood tests and X rays.

Parasites

Parasites make their living at the expense of your cat by ingesting its blood, cells, and tissues. Not only do they damage your cat's health, they can transmit dangerous organisms.

Parasites are divided into two groups: external and internal. External parasites like fleas, ticks, flies, lice, and some kinds of mites live on the skin and in the hair of your cat. Internal parasites such as roundworms and tapeworms live in various locations inside the body.

Fleas are the most common parasites that infest cats and one of the easiest to spot. Symptoms of flea infestation are constant scratching, anemia from blood loss, and changes of the skin including dermatitis, which

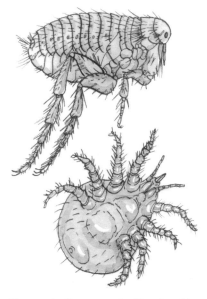

Fleas and mites can make life miserable for your cat.

A flea's bite can transmit micro-scopic tapeworm larvae to your Abyssinian. The larva migrates to the intestine and develops into a long segmented strand that feeds on the nutrients in your cat's digestive system. Segments of the tapeworm strand break off and are elimi-nated with the cat's feces. The segments disintegrate and release embryos, which are eaten by flea larvae, beginning the life cycle again.

causes the cat's skin to itch, redden, and sometimes develop a scabby crust. If you turn your cat over and look at its belly where the hair is sparse, you may see black dots scur-rying around. The fur closest to the skin may show tiny black specks of flea fecal matter known as "coal dust."

Fleas can be hard to eradicate unless you also treat the surrounding environment as well as the cat. If your cat is an outdoor cat, it's getting the fleas from outside and bringing them inside. Fleas can also be passed from cat to cat. The fleas complete their life cycle by laying eggs on your cat and its bedding, and in the carpet of your house.

A multiphasic approach is neces-sary to control the fleas. You must treat your cat for the infestation and the bedding, carpeting, and outside lawn areas, not once but three times at two-week intervals to kill the adult

and the newborn fleas. Be sure not to use a flea product designed for dogs—the label *must* say "safe for cats." Flea products for dogs can kill your cat because they contain a higher level of insecticide.

Ticks are small, eight-legged para-sites that burrow into your cat's skin and suck blood until the tick's body swells to many times its original size. The deer tick, California black-legged tick, and lone star tick can carry Lyme disease, which can be transmitted to cats and humans. Remove ticks promptly by grasping the tick as close to the skin as possible with large tweezers. Twist the tick off, taking care that the head does not remain inside your cat's skin, as this can lead to infection.

Mites are microscopic organisms that burrow into your cat's skin, caus-ing inflammation, hair loss, and irrita-tion. Symptoms include bald patches, dandruff, dermatitis, crust on the skin, and lesions. Because there are several kinds of mites that infest cats, your veterinarian should make the diagnosis. Treatment includes parasiticidal dips and thorough cleaning of the environment.

Blowflies lay their eggs in wounds and matted or soiled hair (as well as in carcasses). Because of this, you should treat even minor wounds promptly. The maggots that hatch from the eggs feed off the flesh of the cat. Symptoms include lesions or ulcers in which the maggots can be seen crawling. Your veterinarian will have to remove the larvae and cleanse the infected area.

Internal parasitic infestation is usually in the form of worms. Tapeworms— long, flat, segmented worms that live in the intestines of their hosts and feed off the nutrients passing through the intestines—are a common parasite in cats. Tapeworms usually do not produce symptoms, but may in severe cases cause weight loss and constant hunger. You may see flat segments of the worm in your cat's feces.

If your cat has fleas, there's a good chance it also has tapeworms, because fleas carry the microscopic larvae of the tapeworm, which they pass on to your cat. Tapeworms are easily treated with Droncit medication.

Roundworms and hookworms, too, live in the intestines and can adversely affect the health of your cat. Hookworms can cause anemia due to blood loss, and a common symptom is black, tarry feces. In severe cases, your cat can die from blood loss. Infestation with roundworms is usually not as serious, not to say your cat should go without being treated. Parasites can cause weakening of your cat's constitution and invite other types of diseases to set in. Both kinds of worms are transmitted by contact with infested soil.

Skin Problems

Skin problems in cats are usually caused by parasites and if the infestation is effectively treated the skin problem will usually improve. Flea allergy dermatitis, caused by an allergic reaction to the flea's bite, is common in cats. However, don't ignore skin conditions, because there could be other causative factors. Your cat could be having an allergic reaction to a new kind of food or something else in the environment.

Ringworm is a common skin problem in cats. Ringworm is caused not by worms but by a fungus that invades the outer layer of the skin, causing patches of hair loss. The patches become red and itchy and develop a crust. Ringworm can be passed to humans, so prompt veterinary treatment is important.

Feline acne is quite common in cats and usually appears on the face and chin. The pores of the skin become clogged, bacteria grow, and blackheads appear. This condition can be treated by feeding your cat on plates rather than in bowls and daily thorough cleansing of the affected area with a veterinarian approved mild soap.

As with any other condition, you should discuss with your veterinarian any changes in your cat's skin or coat.

Periodontal Disease

Abyssinians are particularly prone to gingivitis and other dental problems. Neglected dental disease can contribute to other health problems such as upper respiratory disease, kidney disease, and weakening of the immune system, so vigilant dental care is necessary for your Abyssinian's health.

Kittens have 26 "milk" teeth. The deciduous teeth are replaced by 30 adult teeth by the time a kitten is six months of age. In the healthy adult Abyssinian, the teeth are white and clean. The gums are firm and pink and closely attached to the teeth. The gums may have black pigmentation spots on them as well; this is normal and no cause for concern. If the gums have a bright red line along the gum near the teeth, that's a clear sign that something is wrong.

Gingivitis (Inflammation of the Gums)

It's easy to spot gingivitis in your Abyssinian, if you are observant and know what to look for. If you spot this dental disease early enough, it is relatively easy to treat. The classic signs of gingivitis are tenderness of the gums (your cat may cringe or flinch when you touch the side of its mouth, as when you are petting its whiskers), difficulty or pain when eating, drooling, and bad breath. The gums will look red and swollen, and sometimes will have small whitish ulcers that bleed when touched.

Squamous cell carcinoma, a malignant tumor that affects the gums, tongue, and oral mucous membranes, may appear as lesions that resemble dental ulcers. Dental ulcers may also

If your cat has gingivitis, its teeth will be sensitive. Exercise extreme care when brushing your cat's teeth so it won't learn to dread the process.

be a symptom of pemphigus, a disorder of the immune system, calicivirus, usually associated with upper respiratory disease, and eosinophilic granuloma complex (EGC). Dental ulcers may also be a symptom of other systemic diseases such as kidney disease and diabetes. For this reason you should never ignore dental ulcers. Have a veterinarian examine your cat if you notice any sort of ulcers in the mouth.

The most common cause of gingivitis is the accumulation of plaque and tartar. Plaque is a layer of bacteria trapped in bits of food and saliva that coats the teeth. Tartar develops when plaque mineralizes and hardens, bonding to the tooth. The plaque and tartar can extend under the gum line, causing inflammation and redness. Eventually, the teeth loosen and fall out if the gingivitis is not treated. When the gingivitis gets to this stage, the loose teeth must be removed and the remaining teeth cleaned in order for the inflammation to subside.

Serious Medical Symptoms

If you see any of the following signs, take your cat to the veterinarian right away. These are indications something may be seriously wrong that requires immediate veterinarian intervention:
• repeated vomiting
• refusal to eat or drink
• continued diarrhea
• difficult urination, inability to urinate, blood in urine
• increased urination
• extreme thirst, increased water intake
• increased hunger or food intake
• difficulty in breathing; wheezing, choking
• persistent cough
• seizures
• unresponsiveness, unconsciousness, extreme languor or weakness
• pupils different sizes or unresponsive to light

- disorientation, loss of motor control
- staggering, head tilt, inability to walk normally
- abdominal tenderness or pain
- lumps or swellings
- unexplained weight loss
- sudden blindness or vision disturbances
- coat changes (dullness, dandruff, excessive shedding)
- body held in a hunched position
- discolored tongue
- bleeding/abnormal discharge from a body opening
- bleeding from wounds

Zoonotic Diseases

Humans are much more likely to catch diseases from one another than from their pets. There are, however, a few diseases that can pass from pet to owner. These are called zoonotic diseases. Rabies, bubonic plague, toxoplasmosis, ringworm, cat-scratch fever, chlamydiosis, and Lyme disease have the potential of passing from cats to humans.

Rabies, of course, is a major concern, but you can virtually eliminate the chance of contracting the disease by having your cat vaccinated.

Bubonic plague, the disease that decimated the population of Europe in the mid-1300s, is transmitted by fleas carried by rodents. Cats can transport plague carrying fleas home, and can also contract the disease itself, but it's unlikely. Because plague responds to broad-spectrum antibiotics if treatment is started early in the course of the disease, it's not the terror it was 500 years ago. (Cats, by the way, played a major role in lessening the occurrences of plague in the 1300s by ridding towns of vermin.)

Toxoplasmosis is transmitted through contact with feces and can cause damage to developing embryos. That's the reason women should not clean litter boxes while pregnant and should wear gloves when gardening to avoid contact with contaminated soil. It's not necessary to get rid of your cat if you are pregnant—toxoplasmosis is only transmitted through direct contact with contaminated feces.

If you keep your cat inside (here's another good reason to do so), the chance of contracting any of these diseases is almost nonexistent. Other precautions to take:
- don't feed your cat raw meat.
- always wash your hands after touching any animal.
- clean all scratches and wounds and treat with antiseptic. If infection occurs, see a doctor immediately.
- keep sandboxes and sandpits covered to prevent free roaming cats from using them.
- do not allow young children to handle or clean litter boxes.

HOW-TO:
Caring for Your Sick Abyssinian

If your Abyssinian becomes ill, it's important to know how to care for it at home after the veterinarian has diagnosed the problem and outlined a course of treatment.

Restraint

An injured cat often requires restraint to prevent further injury. Your cat will also need to be restrained in order for you to accomplish necessary treatments. Use the least force necessary to contain the cat, because rough handling is likely to further frighten an already upset cat. Begin with gentle holding and graduate to stronger methods as necessary. Keep calm, and speak softly and reassuringly to your cat.

If your cat is calm, stand or sit the cat on a counter or table and grip the scruff of the neck with one hand. Place your other hand against the chest area of the cat.

Wrapping your Abyssinian in this fashion will prevent the cat from hurting you. The towel should be large enough to wrap around the cat at least twice.

If your cat is frightened and struggling to get away or threatening to scratch you, wrap a towel around the cat so only its head is sticking out. This will allow examination of, or the administration of medication to, the ears, eyes, and mouth. This method also keeps the cat from hurting you, and some cats will even calm down after being wrapped in a towel. Use a towel that is large enough to wrap around the cat at least twice.

If you can't towel a frightened cat because of injury or because the veterinarian needs to make an examination, grip the cat's front and rear legs above the hock. Lay the cat down on its side and hold it on the table. This doesn't hurt the cat and prevents the cat from injuring you.

Medicating Your Cat

Cats are often contrary when it comes to receiving medication. Patience, gentleness, and praise are important to make these unpleasant tasks tolerable for all concerned. Medications can come in several forms: pills, liquids, pastes, and ointments.

Pills and tablets: Many medications come in pill form. Drop the pill as far back in the mouth as possible to get it past the back of the tongue. Give it a gentle push with the tip of your finger if necessary. Then hold your cat's mouth closed and stroke the throat gently to encourage your cat to swallow while praising the cat's exemplary behavior.

It helps to have an assistant help hold the cat while you give the medication. If the pill is large, you can smear the pill

Gently pry open the cat's mouth and tilt the head back. Drop the pill as far back in the mouth as possible to get it past the back of the tongue. Give it a gentle push if necessary.

with butter to help it slide down more easily.

Do not crush the pills to aid administration without first checking with your veterinarian.

Liquids: Give liquid medications with an eyedropper or syringe (without the needle attached). Use the same restraining method used to pill your cat and administer the liquid two to three drops at a time. Allow the cat to swallow before giving more.

You can also try mixing the medication in a *small amount* of your cat's favorite food; how-

Gently hold the cat's mouth closed until it has swallowed.

ever, some medications are too noticeable or bitter for this to be effective. If you try this method, be sure the cat eats all of the medicated treat, and that your other cats do not share the food. Talk to your veterinarian before attempting this technique. This method is not appropriate for all medications.

Ointments: External ointments are prescribed for various skin conditions. Rub the ointment into the affected area thoroughly. Keep your cat from licking the area for at least 15 minutes—hold the cat or distract it by feeding, grooming, or playing with it. Some ointments are intentionally bitter to discourage cats from licking them off; ask your veterinarian.

Injections: Trained veterinary personnel usually give injections. However, some diseases such as feline diabetes require regular injections that you can give at home. Ask your veterinarian to instruct you before you attempt to give an injection to your cat.

Applying Ointment to Your Cat's Eyes

Treatment of certain conditions, such as conjunctivitis (see page 67), require the application of eye ointment. Tilt the cat's head up slightly. Keep the tube of medication parallel with the eye to avoid poking the eye. Gently squeeze a line of ointment onto the eyeball. Hold the eye closed for a few moments by pushing gently up on the cheek; this will give the medication time to melt.

Applying Ear Drops

Your veterinarian may prescribe ear drops for various ear

Tilt the cat's head back and administer the liquid two to three drops at a time. Allow the cat to swallow. If the cat tries to spit out the medication, hold the mouth closed until the cat swallows.

conditions such as ear mites and infections. Have an assistant hold the cat while you drop the prescribed number of drops into the ear canal. Do not poke the applicator deep into the ear canal as that can cause damage. Massage the ear gently afterwards to spread the medication.

Taking Your Cat's Temperature

It's helpful to be able to determine your cat's temperature when you suspect the cat is not feeling well. A healthy cat's temperature is 100 to 102.5°F (37.8–39°C). A temperature of 105°F (40.6°C) is considered a danger sign. Use a human rectal thermometer (not an oral one), and shake it down to 96°F (35.6°C) or lower. Lubricate it with KY Jelly or petroleum gel. Have an assistant gently hold the cat by placing one restraining hand on the chest and the other hand on the scruff. While the cat is being held, lift the cat's tail and gently and slowly insert the thermometer into the anus until

about an inch (2.5 cm) of the thermometer is inside the cat. Leave it in place for one to two minutes, then remove and read. *Never* attempt to take a cat's temperature orally; the cat will likely bite down and may shatter the thermometer.

Feeding Your Sick Cat

Cats who are ill will often lose their appetites (be off their feed). Smell is also very important to cats' feeding habits, so a congested cat may eat less or not at all. Cleaning the nose of nasal discharge with a cotton ball moistened with water may help.

Eating and drinking are important to your cat's recovery. You may have to assist your cat when it is ill. Feeding your cat pungent fish such as tuna may help; you can also try adding the water or oil from canned tuna to your cat's food to increase its interest in eating. If all else fails, there are a variety of paste and liquid foods available at pet supply stores and your veterinarian's office.

Give paste foods by holding your cat in the "pilling position." Tip the head up slightly, hold the mouth open, and place a strip of paste into the mouth. The cat will usually attempt to swallow. Do not release the head because the cat may spit out the food or shake its head.

You can give liquid foods or water by using the same method used to give liquid medication. Some conditions will cause your cat to become dehydrated and your veterinarian may suggest that you administer water. Flavoring the water with tuna juice may help make the water more palatable.

Grooming

Cats are naturally clean animals and devote a good portion of their day to grooming themselves. The cat's tongue is covered with hooked, backward-pointing scales called papillae. These scales make the tongue good for combing the fur and skin. Some breeds, like the longhaired Persian, need quite a bit of help from their humans to keep looking sharp. The Abyssinian, with its short, compact coat, is easy to take care of.

That's not to say you don't need to groom your Abyssinian. A regular grooming program is good for a cat's health. Grooming removes dead hair that can form hair balls in a cat's stomach (as well as covering your couch), gets rid of dead skin and dander, stimulates the skin, tones muscles, and encourages blood circulation. It is also a good opportunity to examine your cat for developing health problems and attend to them in their early stages.

Grooming involves more than combing a cat's fur. The cat's nails, ears, eyes, and teeth need attention, too. Grooming can be a pleasant experience for you and your feline friend, if you train the cat to tolerate grooming when it is young. Preferably, you should start a grooming program when your cat is three months old. Your cat will get to expect and even enjoy its grooming sessions with its favorite human.

Grooming the show Abyssinian is more detailed, because the cat must look its absolute best for the show ring. Most exhibitors bathe their cats three or four days before shows, and use products such as coat conditioners to make the coat soft and manageable. They meticulously comb their cats and clean the eyes, ears, and face with cotton balls and swabs. Many exhibitors end by stroking the cat, as the natural oils on their hands makes the hair shine, or rubbing the cat with a silk scarf to polish the fur just before entering the ring.

Coat Care

Unless you will be showing your Abyssinian, the cat will do fine with a once-a-week grooming. Pick a spot such as the bathroom, back porch, or other enclosed area to make cleanup easier if the fur flies. Before taking the cat to the grooming area, have all the grooming supplies ready and in place.

Grooming supplies

Abyssinians, like most cats, spend considerable time keeping themselves well groomed.

Then you won't have to run off to find something and come back to find the cat hiding under the bed or eating the shampoo. Keeping all the grooming supplies in a caddy is a convenient way to keep them together and make transportation easy.

Before beginning, run your hands over the cat's body, feeling for any swellings, lumps, growths, or abscesses. Check for signs of tenderness, thin or bald spots, the "coal dust" of fleas, and excessive flaking of the skin. Feel the tail gently for lumps, and the belly too, if the cat will hold still for it. Some cats react negatively to having their tummies touched and may try to scratch.

Comb your Abyssinian's fur with a fine-toothed metal comb. This kind of comb removes dead and loose hairs, catches fleas and flea dirt, and doesn't damage the Abyssinian's beautiful fur. Don't use rubber, wire, or "slicker" type brushes as these can damage the coat.

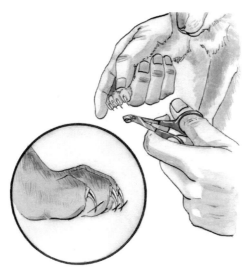

Hold the cat firmly in your lap and press the pad of the foot gently to extend the claws. Clip the white area of the nail.

Start at the head and work down to the tail, combing with the lie of the fur. Comb gently and talk softly to your cat. Most Abyssinians like to be combed and will arch up against your hand and rub their heads against you in an ecstasy of delight. Cats are accustomed to being groomed by their mothers. Because your cat sees you as its surrogate "cat-mom" or "cat-dad," it should tolerate grooming without too much protest.

If the cat doesn't like being combed, if it tries to run away or behaves aggressively toward you, try limiting the grooming sessions to a few minutes. Slowly work up to longer sessions. It could be that you're being too rough. Save the procedures that your cat dislikes—such as nail clipping or bathing—for separate grooming sessions so it doesn't associate its general grooming with these unpleasant activities.

If you wish, you can finish up the grooming session by going over the coat with a soft bristle brush to remove any remaining loose hairs. If you are going to treat your Abyssinian to a dose of a petrolatum product such as Kittymalt or Petromalt to help prevent hair balls, this is a good time to do so. Because these products are usually given by smearing a dab onto the paw or side of the mouth and allowing the cat to lick it off, your cat will pick up less fur in the process if you dispense the medication after grooming.

Nail Care

Trim your Abyssinian's toenails every two to three weeks. Not only does this save on the wear and tear of your furniture, it reduces the risk of your cat injuring you and your other pets.

An indoor cat's claws do not wear down as much as an outdoor cat's claws will, and can grow into the pad of the paw. You can prevent this with regular trimming.

Use either nail clippers designed for cats or heavy-duty human nail clippers. With the cat held in your lap, hold one paw and *gently* apply pressure on the paw to make the claws extend. Clip off the white part of the nail, being careful not to cut into the pink "quick" of the nail. The quick is rich with nerve endings and hurts very badly if cut—probably akin to getting a sliver rammed under the fingernail. Don't cut the white part of the nail any closer than 0.1 inch (2.5 mm) from the quick. Just one experience with the "cruelest cut of all" and your cat will not react well to having its nails clipped from then on. If you've never trimmed a cat's nails, you may want to ask your veterinarian to show you how.

If the cat reacts badly to having its nails cut, enlist the help of a partner to get the job done. Or catch the cat just after it has awakened from its afternoon nap and is sleepy. Be gentle, be kind, and your Abyssinian will learn to accept nail trimming as just another of those incomprehensible things that humans do.

Ear and Eye Care

As described in the previous chapter, a cat's eyes should be free of discharge and inflammation, and its haws should not protrude. These can be signs of serious illness. However, the area around the eyes (particularly under the eyes) can accumulate dirt, dried tears, and sleep residue. During

When cleaning the ears, do not push the swab or cotton ball into the ear canal.

the weekly grooming session, or whenever the cat seems to need a bit of extra attention, wipe the eyes clean with a cotton ball moistened with warm (not hot) water.

The ears of a normal, healthy cat should be clean and free of excessive waxy discharge. A healthy cat's ears shouldn't require much attention. Look inside the flap. Clean any dirt or excessive wax buildup from the outer ear area with a cotton ball or swab moistened with a few drops of olive oil. Don't poke the swab or any object into the ear canal.

Mature red Abyssinian. The Abyssinian color red is called "sorrel" by some cat associations.

Red Abyssinian. Note the characteristic "M" on the forehead. According to folklore, this tabby marking is a gift from the Virgin Mary.

HOW-TO:
Bathing Your Abyssinian

Why Bathe Your Cat?

The jury is still out on bathing cats. Some people believe that bathing cats is unnecessary and indeed can be harmful to cats' health. Others believe that cats benefit from regular bathing. Personally, I don't believe that bathing a normal, healthy cat causes any harm, but you must make the final decision. There are many factors to consider, and you may wish to consult your veterinarian if you have concerns.

An indoor-outdoor cat will almost certainly need periodic baths. If kept inside, the cat may go longer without needing bathing. However, if a cat has a continuous problem with parasites or skin allergies, is a lazy groomer, or has a weight problem and cannot groom itself properly, regular bathing will certainly be helpful.

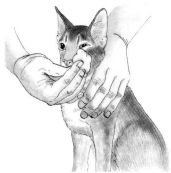

Wipe the face clean with a cotton ball moistened with warm water. This will remove dirt, "sleep" residue, and dried tears. Do not use soap or any material that might scratch the eye.

Stud tail, an accumulation of waxy debris on the base of the tail caused by hyperactive sebaceous glands, is fairly common, particularly in unneutered male cats. Regular bathing will reduce these secretions and prevent the hair loss, irritation, and inflammation that can accompany this condition.

Routine bathing of your cat may benefit *your* health as well. Recent studies have shown that regular bathing of cats can remove a good percentage of the dander that triggers allergic reactions in humans.

Overcoming Your Cat's Fear

Help your cat overcome the fear of being bathed by establishing a routine early in the cat's life, and by gaining the cat's trust. Cats who react violently to bath time are the ones bathed infrequently. It must seem that every now and then their beloved human companions go berserk and try to drown them. Cats are creatures of habit. If you start bathing and grooming cats when they are young, they will learn to tolerate these procedures much better than if you bathe and groom them only once in a while.

Where to Bathe

You can bathe the cat in the bathtub, bathroom sink, or the kitchen sink. Some veterinarians recommend using a kitchen sink equipped with a spray hose attachment. You have more control over the cat when you're standing up than when bending over. It's also easier on your back. You can buy an inexpensive rubber spray hose that

If a cat becomes uncontrollable, hold the cat down by gripping the nape of the neck. This should cause the cat to stop struggling.

attaches to the kitchen or bathroom faucet. Your local bath or hardware supply store should carry them. If your sink is too small or your cat too big, use the tub. Be sure you can close off the chosen area. Chasing a wet, scared, slippery cat over the sofa and under the bed isn't any fun.

Before bathing a cat, trim its nails (giving blood is admirable only when you're donating to the Red Cross). Comb the cat thoroughly to keep as much hair as possible from going down the drain.

Use the Correct Shampoo

You can use a flea control shampoo, a quality cat shampoo, or a gentle, protein-enriched shampoo designed for humans. Baby shampoo is fine. Don't use ordinary dish soap, which can dry out the cat's skin, and never use flea shampoo designed for dogs. The concentration of insecticide in dog shampoo can be harmful or even fatal to cats.

How to Bathe

To prevent water and soap from getting into the cat's ears,

Hold the spray attachment close to the cat's body. Never spray the cat's face or head.

plug the ears with cotton. You can also put a drop or two of mineral oil in each eye to protect the eyes from the soap.

If bathing the cat in the tub, put two rectangular basins inside the tub and fill them with water. One is for getting the cat wet, and the second is for rinsing. If using a sink, use a hose attachment to wet and rinse.

If using the tub method, fill the basins with water before you put the cat in. The sound of the water is alarming to cats. Keep the water at around the cat's normal body temperature of 101.4°F (38.5°C), or lower. Dip your elbow into the water to make sure it's not too hot before putting in the cat. Continue to monitor the water temperature as you go.

If using a hose attachment, preheat the water before putting the cat in the sink. Be sure to test the temperature of the water. Hold the head of the hose close to the cat's body when wetting the cat to cut down on the splashing sound. Never spray the head, face, or ears.

Put the cat into the sink or tub with its back facing you so it won't scratch you if it strikes out or struggles. Hold the cat in place by applying gentle pressure to the shoulder area. A rubber mat is helpful to keep the cat from slipping.

If the cat becomes uncontrollable, hold the cat by gripping the nape of the neck and *pushing down*. Gripping the nape should cause the cat to freeze instinctively, because queens carry their young in this fashion. Never lift a full grown cat by the nape—that can cause serious injury.

While bathing the cat, try to remain calm and never yell or strike at your cat. That will frighten the cat further. A panicked cat could seriously injure you. Talk soothingly; the cat doesn't understand what you're doing and needs reassurance.

Wet the cat's coat thoroughly by running your hand through the grain of the coat, but do not wet above the neckline. If the cat has a flea problem, wet and shampoo the neck area first to keep the fleas from escaping up the neck and onto the head. Never dunk a cat's head under the water, or spray water onto your cat's head.

When the cat is completely wet, lift it out of the water and set it in the tub. Apply the shampoo, using the squeeze bottle. Work the shampoo into the coat well. Don't neglect the legs, feet, and tail. Be very careful not to bend the tail tip; the bones are delicate and break easily.

Put the cat into the first basin again to rinse. Try to massage as much soap out of the fur as possible, and then put the cat into the second basin. It's very important to get all the soap out of the fur, because your cat will groom after its bath and will ingest any remaining soap. Continue to rinse until the fur has lost the slick, soapy feel and the rinse water runs off clear. If necessary, empty the first basin and fill it with clean water again for an additional rinsing.

After you have rinsed the cat thoroughly, run your hands down its body to remove excess water. Wrap your cat in a terry towel with just the head showing, and use a damp terry washcloth to clean the head, face, and chin. Change the towel and dry the cat well by patting the fur with the towel. Use a third towel if necessary.

When the coat is as dry as possible, leave the cat in the enclosed area to sulk and groom itself. Don't let the cat into drafty areas or outside until it is completely dry. Most cats will groom continuously until they are dry again. Remember to remove the cotton plugs from the ears.

After you have thoroughly rinsed your cat's coat, towel it dry with a warm terry towel. Change towels once or twice as necessary. Then allow your cat to put its coat back in place and finish the drying process on its own.

Sexual Behavior

Cats, like all creatures that reproduce sexually, are driven by their instinctual need to mate. To better understand feline sexual drives, it's important to take a look at the cycles that influence hormone levels and cats' sexual behavior.

The Queen's Heat

A breeding female cat, called a queen, will usually go into her first heat between eight and ten months of age. The Abyssinian, however, is a late bloomer—the onset of estrus (the period in which the queen is sexually receptive) comes in the eleventh or twelfth month, sometimes even later. The queen's estrus cycles are seasonal, and in the Northern Hemisphere breeding begins as early as January and usually ends in October. (In the Southern Hemisphere the cycle is exactly the opposite.)

Because the photocycle regulates a cat's heat, cats ordinarily do not go into heat from October through December, but there can be exceptions to that rule. Indoor-only cats can go into heat out of season. The onset of ovarian follicle growth is caused by the effect of increased light stimulation on the hypothalamus. More simply, when the days get longer, the brain tells the body it's time to mate.

Estrus usually lasts for five to eight days, but can go as long as twenty. Estrus comes in three stages: proestrus (the period just before estrus), estrus (when the cat is ready to copulate), and interestrus (the period of ovarian and sexual inactivity that follows estrus, and that normally lasts from a number of days to three or four weeks).

In proestrus, the queen may become more affectionate to you and to the other animals in the household. She may want to be petted more often, to sit in your lap, or just to be near you. It's also possible that you will not notice any change in the cat's behavior during this period. Proestrus typically lasts only a day or so.

When estrus begins, it's usually obvious. The queen will meow and howl insistently; this distinctive sound is called "calling." She will roll on the ground and rub up against you and your possessions.

The queen may assume the mating position called lordosis; she will crouch down low with her back swayed, her tail held to one side, and tread with her rear feet while bellowing at the top of her lungs. She may also pace back and forth and seem restless and agitated. If allowed outside, the queen may disappear for several days, and likely come home pregnant. Queens can go into heat several times during the yearly cycle if copulation and impregnation do not occur. Having a cat prowling around yowling for a mate is distracting at best. Spay your cat if you do not intend to breed her. Spaying removes the annoying behaviors associated with estrus and is kinder to the cat. It's cruel to allow her to suffer repeated sexual frustration.

The Tom's Rut

Unlike females, unneutered adult males (toms) are in a constant state of sexual readiness. Males reach puberty

Mature ruddy Abyssinian. Note the heavier jowls and the regal expression.

and begin producing androgen (sex hormones) at around nine months of age. From then on, they spend most of their time searching out willing females and defending their territory from other males. The tom's habit of marking his territory by spraying is sexual in origin. It is dependent on the presence of male sex hormones, which is why neutering curbs this behavior.

When a queen goes into estrus, she produces high levels of pheromones with which to attract her mate. Toms can perceive these olfactory signals from a long distance away. This is how the neighborhood toms know to line up on the doorstep when your cat is in heat. The tom shows his sexual readiness by pacing back and forth, licking his penis, and yowling.

Tom cats, as a general rule, are not particular about whom they mate with; breed, age, health, appearance, or familial relationship are not considerations for a sexually ready tom. Tom cats will readily mate with their grandmothers, mothers, sisters, and daughters.

Mating

When a tom senses a female in heat, he goes through a ritual courting in which the male approaches and calls to his chosen love. At first, the queen may snarl and strike out at the male.

The tom accepts this passively, drawing to one side and watching the female. The male may make plaintive yowls called "singing," as if to persuade the female to be more reasonable.

When the female is ready to allow copulation, she gives an "appeasement cry" to show that she is sexually receptive. She assumes the lordotic posture with her tail to one side to allow easier penetration by the tom. The tom immediately mounts the queen by grasping the back of her neck in his teeth. He places his forelegs over her shoulders and positions himself by straddling her pelvic area and paddling against her sides with his feet (he may actually step on her). This causes the queen to sway her back and raise her vulva. When the position is correct, the tom inserts his penis into the queen's vagina. Ejaculation is almost immediate.

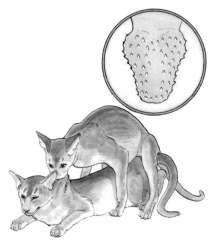

Abyssinians mating: the male quickly mounts the female and grips the back of her neck. The barbs on the penis are thought to stimulate ovulation.

When the tom withdraws, the queen lets out a high-pitched, distinctive scream, which shows that the mating has been successful. Researchers used to think the scream was caused by the pain of withdrawal, because the tom's penis is covered with spiny barbs that point toward the base of the penis. That is probably not the reason, because the copulatory scream can be provoked by insertion of a smooth rod and by certain acupressure techniques used to end estrus. The purpose of the barbs may be to help the male maintain penetration, or they may help provoke ovulation. No one knows for sure. They could be responsible for the aggressive reaction of the female following mating—that would certainly be understandable.

If the male does not disengage and move away promptly, the female will turn, snarl, and strike out at the tom. Following copulation, the queen rolls on the ground and licks her genitalia. The tom withdraws a short distance away and watches the female. After an intermission of several minutes to several hours, the mating cycle repeats. Cats can copulate many times within the estrus period.

Felines are "induced ovulators." Copulation must take place for ovulation to occur. Copulation evokes a release of luteinizing hormone into the pituitary, which triggers ovulation. Ovulation ordinarily takes place 24 to 30 hours after copulation has occurred. It's important not to allow a breeding queen outside even after mating has taken place. It is possible for different toms to father kittens within a single litter, and you can end up with some mixed, unpedigreed kittens in what you thought would be an all-purebred litter.

Breeding Your Abyssinian

Why Breed Your Abyssinian?

Before deciding to take on the responsibility of breeding your Abyssinian, it's important to weigh the considerations carefully. Although the idea of raising beautiful kittens to provide joy to loving, responsible homes while making tons of money is certainly attractive, it's not as easy as it sounds. Breeding cats is time-consuming, difficult, and frustrating, and it can be heartbreaking. And instead of making money, you are much more likely to invest thousands more than you earn. Very few reputable breeders break even and even fewer profit.

Another factor to consider is the domestic animal over-population problem. There aren't enough good homes for all the deserving cats and dogs. Watching an endless progression of cats and dogs being euthanized is frustrating and heartbreaking for animal lovers like you and me, and for the caring people who staff the animal shelters. You should not become a breeder without looking at the cat population problem and accepting your responsibilities in promoting conscientious cat ownership. If you do decide to take the breeding plunge, make a vow to contribute to the welfare and well-being of your feline friends, as well as to the purity and perfection of the Abyssinian bloodline. Start with a small number of high-quality cats—the absolute best you can afford—and dedicate yourself to producing a small number of high-quality kittens.

Before becoming a breeder, ask yourself these questions:
- Can I afford all the costs involved, including stud fees, veterinary care, advertising, vaccinations, cat food, litter, cat accessories, and so on?
- Do I have the time and energy necessary to give all my cats quality care?
- Do I have a goal in mind for my breeding program, and am I concerned more with quality than quantity?
- Am I prepared to test my goals and achievements by exhibiting my cats?
- Do I have the emotional detachment necessary to evaluate my breeding stock objectively and cull those that don't measure up?
- Will I find loving homes for all kittens, and make sure that the pet-quality kittens are spayed or neutered?
- Will I work hard to keep my breeding stock free from infectious diseases, parasites, and genetic disorders?

Genetics

In order to maintain an effective breeding program, a basic understanding of genetics is essential.

The feline's body, like your body, is composed of individual cells. Within each cell is a nucleus, which contains the genetic material that specifies the precise structure of the animal. Within the nucleus are threadlike chromosomes, which are made of the nucleic acid deoxyribonucleic acid (DNA). Ribonucleic acid (RNA) is similar to DNA but is formed in shorter molecules and acts as DNA's "messengers." RNA molecules construct the strings of amino acids that form proteins.

Felines have 19 pairs of chromosomes (38 total), which exist inside each cell nucleus. Cats inherit one set of chromosomes from each parent—one set of 19 chromosomes from the mother's egg cell and one set of 19 from the father's sperm cell. These chromosomes are responsible for the determination and transmission of all the hereditary characteristics such as eye color, hair length, and hair color.

One set of cells is constructed differently from the rest—the sex cells (called eggs in the female, and sperm in the male), which contain 19 single or unpaired chromosomes. The female sex chromosome is noted as X, and the male is noted as Y. When

Ruddy Abyssinian.

a sperm fertilizes an egg, the resulting progeny cell then acquires 19 chromosomes from each parent cell, resulting in a total of 38 paired chromosomes.

The sex chromosomes determine the sex of the cat. The female always has two X chromosomes and the male has one X and one Y chromosome (XX = female, XY = male). If a kitten inherits an X chromosome from its mother and an X from its father, the kitten will be female. If, however, it inherits the Y chromosome from the father, the kitten will be male. Roughly half of a male's sperm cells will bear an X, and half will bear a Y. Genes that are carried on female X chromosomes are sex-linked genes.

Chromosomes are made of the building blocks of life—genes. Each gene provides the genetic "blueprint" necessary for the cell to produce a single protein. Each protein product influences the structure, function, metabolism, and embryonic differentiation of the body's cells. Each chromosome is made of several thousand individual genes. The genes are always found at specific places along the chromosome. The genetic makeup of a cat is called the genotype.

Changes in the genetic code create mutations. If the change occurs in a gamete (eggs or sperm), the offspring will carry that genetic mutation, and may show the effect of the altered cell product. The original form of the gene is called the wildtype or wild form, whereas all the new mutated forms of the gene are called alleles.

When both copies of a particular gene are identical (in other words, when the cat receives the same gene from both parents), we say that the cat is homozygous for the trait governed by that gene. That trait will, of course, be expressed. If the cat has two different alleles for a particular gene, the cat is called heterozygous for that trait.

This can express itself in a variety of ways, depending on the kind of cell product that is being produced by the gene and the kind of change produced by the alleles. Sometimes both alleles can express themselves and this is called nondominance or codominance. In other cases, the effect of one allele masks the effect of the other allele. The expressed gene is called dominant, and the gene that is present but not expressed is called recessive.

Dominant genes determine the animal's phenotype (physical appearance). For example, the ruddy color in the Abyssinian is dominant over the other coat colors. If an Abyssinian carries the gene for ruddy it will be expressed, because it is dominant over any other color. In other words, if the cat is not ruddy, it cannot have the gene for ruddy. Abyssinian red, however, is a dilution (a softer, paler version) of ruddy, and therefore is recessive. The gene for red can be present but unexpressed because it is masked by the ruddy gene. Only if the cat has received the red gene from both parents will the cat be red. (The red color in the Abyssinian is a dilution rather than a sex-linked color, unlike the orange gene that is responsible for the red color in other breeds.)

In order to more easily keep track of all this, a system of internationally recognized symbols has been established. A sampling of the symbols appears on page 91. Capital letters indicate dominant genes whereas lowercase letters represent recessive genes.

Genetically, the Abyssinian coat pattern is a different form of the tabby pattern. The pattern is called agouti and means that instead of tabby striping, each hair is banded in two or more alternating colors. It is thought that the agouti pattern developed as a form of camouflaging.

The agouti pattern is inherited as an incomplete dominant to the striped

Blue Abyssinian.

tabby. It is not completely dominant over the tabby pattern, which is why you can see faint tabby barring on the face and sometimes on the chest, legs, and tail for the Abyssinian. (The T^a Abyssinian gene does not fully mask the T tabby gene.) Because tabby barring on the chest, legs and tail is a fault in the show Abyssinian, breeders do their best to eliminate this barring in their cats.

Mendelian Genetics

Gregor Mendel (1822–1884), an Austrian monk and naturalist, was the first person to develop a clear understanding of how simple traits are inherited. The amazing thing is that he figured all this out before it was understood how chromosomes functioned.

Mendel's First Law: If two animals of pure strain but with different genes for one trait are mated, all the first-generation offspring are hybrids and look alike in respect to this trait. For example: If you mate a homozygous ruddy male with a homozygous red female, all of the kittens would be ruddy because ruddy is dominant over red, but all the kittens would carry the recessive gene for red. This is easier to visualize by using what's called a Punnett square:

Sire → Dam ↓	ruddy	
red	R	R
r	Rr	Rr
r	Rr	Rr

Mendel's Second Law: If you mate the ruddy, heterozygous kittens (Rr) together, the characteristics of both their grandparents will show up again in pure (homozygous) form. These second-generation kittens do not all look alike and will have different combinations of genes. They will exhibit three different gene patterns in a ratio of 1:2:1—one homozygous ruddy, one homozygous red, and two heterozygous ruddy carrying red:

Sire → Dam ↓	ruddy carrying red	
ruddy carrying red	R	r
R	RR	Rr
r	rR	rr

By using Punnett squares, you can theoretically calculate the possible genetic outcome of any given mating. All you need to know is the genetic makeup of the parent cats—now, that's the hard part.

Sire → Dam ↓	ruddy	
blue	R	R
b	Rb	Rb
b	Rb	Rb

Sire → Dam ↓	ruddy carrying blue	
ruddy carrying blue	R	b
R	RR	Rb
b	bR	bb

See the phenotype color inheritance chart on page 108 for detailed information on inheritance of the four Abyssinian colors.

To determine the genotype of your cat, you can use two sources of information. The first is the cat's pedigree, which provides you with a five-generation record of your cat's ancestors. For example, if your cat is ruddy, and you see on your cat's pedigree that one of it's parents was red, you know that your cat carries the red gene.

When reading the pedigree, you'll notice that the first part of the name of the cat refers to the cattery where the cat was bred, and the last part of the name refers to the current owner's cattery name. For example, if a cat is named Sallyho's Ruddy Buddy of Punkin's Cats, you know that the cattery's name is Sallyho, the cat's official name is Ruddy Buddy, and the current owner's cattery name is Punkin's Cats. If the cat is a champion or grand champion, the name will be prefixed by Ch. or Gr. Ch.

The second source of information comes from the kind of kittens your cat

Internationally Recognized Gene Symbols

Symbol	Designation
A	Agouti tabby pattern
a	Non-agouti
T^a	Abyssinian pattern
T	Striped tabby pattern
C	Full color
D	Intense color
d	Dilute color
B	Black
b	Chocolate brown
b^1	Red-brown
T^aT^a	Ruddy Abyssinian
$b^1b^1T^aT^a$	Red Abyssinian
ddT^aT^a	Blue Abyssinian
$b^1b^1ddT^aT^a$	Fawn Abyssinian

produces. For example, if you breed a ruddy to a ruddy and produce a red kitten, then you know that both parents carry the recessive red gene, because that kitten must get the red gene from both parents to be red. You also can figure that some of the ruddy kittens in that litter will also carry the red gene.

Breeding Programs

There are four major types of breeding practices used to develop and improve a cat's bloodlines: inbreeding, linebreeding, linecrossing (also called outcrossing), and crossbreeding.

Inbreeding involves mating closely related cats to one another: for example; father to daughter, mother to son, brother to sister, first cousin to first cousin. Inbreeding is used to "set" particular desired traits into the bloodline of a cat—to make the cats more uniform by creating more homozygous gene pairs. This sounds good in theory; however, detrimental alleles will also become established in the lines by use of this method, causing medical problems and general loss of vigor. To avoid acquiring detrimental

genes in their Abyssinian bloodlines, breeders must start with the widest gene pool possible.

Linebreeding (also called moderate inbreeding), involves breeding cats that share the same bloodline but that are not as closely related as with inbreeding; for example, mating a cat to its great-grandparent, second or third cousin, great aunt or uncle. The common ancestors are farther back along the pedigree, but the pedigree of a linebred kitten will show the same select cats several times in its ancestry. This method is used to concentrate the good qualities of outstanding examples of the breed without resorting to direct inbreeding. In breeds with a large gene pool like the Abyssinian, linebreeding is usually not damaging.

Linecrossing or **outcrossing** involves mating together two good examples of the breed that do not share a bloodline in order to profit from the good qualities of both lines. Ideally, the bloodlines used should not have the same strengths and weaknesses. For example, if you were to breed a cat from a bloodline known for its outstanding eye color together with a cat from a bloodline known for its outstanding head shape, a small percentage of the offspring produced would have both outstanding eye color and head shape.

Crossbreeding involves mating cats from different breeds. It is used to create new breeds of cats. For example, the Somali was most likely the product of an original cross between an Abyssinian and a longhaired cat. Because there is no allowable outcrossing for the Abyssinian (the Abyssinian gene pool is closed), this method is not used in Abyssinian breeding programs.

The Basics of Breeding

Because Abyssinians tend to mature later than some breeds, you should not breed your queen until she is at least one year old. If you breed her earlier, she may never achieve her full size, as the nutrients needed for her growth will be diverted for reproduction.

Finding a Queen

When starting a cattery, it's very important to start with the highest quality queen or queens that you can buy. Ideally, you should purchase your queen from a well-established and reputable breeder who has a proven track record of producing high-quality kittens. Well-established breeders, however, will rarely sell queens to novice breeders. Reputable breeders are extremely selective in placing their breed-quality females, and the demand (and price) for show- and breed-quality queens is high.

Most reputable breeders want to place their best cats with breeders with proven track records who are dedicated to improving the breed.

Fawn Abyssinian.

"Backyard" and "kitten mill" breeders will sell to anyone who will pay their price, but their stock is likely to be poor examples of the breed, and may have genetic, health, or behavioral problems as well.

The best way to obtain a high-quality queen is by going to shows and getting to know breeders; buying a show-quality altered male and making the show rounds is a good way to accomplish this. The experience you gain from showing and being around breeders and exhibitors will be invaluable. Make yourself more knowledgeable by talking with breeders, judges, and veterinarians, by reading all you can about Abyssinians and breeding cats, and by joining an Abyssinian cat club.

After you make initial contacts, try to find a breeder who is willing to become your "mentor," or who is willing to co-own a good-quality queen with you. (A co-owning breeder will want to exercise control over the sale of any resulting kittens.) This method is time-consuming, but your results will be far better and much less frustrating than if you start with mediocre stock.

Finding a Stud

Because you probably will not be keeping a whole male in your cattery, you will need to arrange a date for your Abyssinian queen. This form of "planned parenthood" is common among breeders, and many established breeders offer stud service.

The queen should be at least twelve months old before you attempt to breed her, and you really should wait longer. Before breeding your queen, she should have a veterinary examination.

The basic requirement of the stud is that he is, of course, a purebred, registered Abyssinian and that he is "proven" (sired at least one litter). If the stud is not registered, the kittens will not be registrable regardless of the quality and qualifications of the queen.

Be sure to ask to see the certificate of registration, which will tell you the cat's name, date of birth, breed, color, sire and dam's names, registration number, and cattery name.

Select a stud that is a champion or grand champion, because this is proof the judges have found the cat to be an excellent example of the breed. When you are beginning, it's difficult to ascertain a stud's quality on your own.

If this is your queen's first mating, select an experienced stud. Be prepared for the breeder to reject the match if your queen is not a champion or grand champion, or if the pedigrees of the two show a potential mismatch.

When selecting a stud, you should keep in mind the qualities that are important to you. When doing this, study the standard for the breed and see where your cat meets the standard and where it could improve. Keep in mind the areas that need improving when you select the stud.

Consider the personality of the cat, which is just as important as how the cat looks. Personality traits have a genetic base just as color and conformation do. If your line of cats is gorgeous to look at but they all hide under the bed whenever you come near or are so hyperactive that they run around the house without touching the floors, you've done yourself and the Abyssinian breed no favors.

If you cannot find an Abyssinian stud in your area or wish the services of a high-quality stud in a specific bloodline elsewhere, ask the breeder to send pictures of the stud. Most breeders have pictures available. If possible, arrange to meet the breeder and his or her stud before you finalize the arrangements. Ask to see the stud's current vaccination records and test results that show the cat is free of feline leukemia virus (FeLV). Combine that with your own powers of observation—is the stud a friendly, affection- ate cat or an aggressive, fearful one? Does its coat look healthy and are its eyes and nose free of discharge? Is the cattery clean and well-maintained? Use the same guidelines for selecting a stud as you did when you selected your cat (see page 17).

The Stud Fee

Depending on the stud you pick for your queen, the stud fee could be as low as a few hundred dollars, or it could be much higher for an outstanding, well-known grand champion. (If you think that's bad, be grateful you're not breeding racehorses.) The owner sets the fee depending on the merit and value of the stud. The fee usually includes a return visit if the queen does not conceive the first time. It's best to have a stud contract spelling out the terms. Be sure the agreement includes the owner's willingness to sign the registration forms when the kittens are born and to arrange a sec- ond coupling if the mating does not occur as scheduled. (Sometimes a queen will reject the studly male you've selected for her, regardless of his impeccable pedigree.)

These week-old Abyssinian kittens do not yet have their eyes open.

You will almost always take the queen to the stud for the mating, because the queen will not then feel that she must protect her territory from the unfamiliar male. The trauma of traveling, however, can sometimes interfere with the heat cycle. Wait until the queen is in the second day of heat to transport her.

When you bring the pair together for mating, you should cage them separately but put them near one another so they can see and smell each other. When they seem ready, you can put them in a room together, but stand ready to interfere in case the queen should attack the male or (less common) vice versa. Soon, however, nature should take its course.

The pair will mate many times over the next three days. You or the owner of the stud should observe at least a couple of the pairings to be sure mating has taken place.

After you bring the queen home, she will probably remain in heat for a few more days. Do not let her outside or allow contact with any other whole males. Different fathers can sire kittens within the same litter and you don't want to end up with a mixed litter of kittens after all that.

Pregnancy and Birth

If the mating didn't "take," the queen will go back into heat in one to three weeks. If she is pregnant, her nipples will become erect and gradually turn a darker shade of pink; this takes place about three weeks after conception. She may develop morning sickness (yes, cats go through it too), and she may become more affectionate to you, in response to the change in hormone levels in her body.

She will also want to eat even more than usual. Nutrition is particularly important during this time; be sure to feed her a food recommended for pregnant queens. Make sure she gets plenty of protein, calcium, and phosphorus (see Nutrition, page 46). If you have concerns, consult your veterinarian. Avoid medications except those recommended by your veterinarian.

Be sure to keep careful records of the date of conception and subsequent developments. This is important in determining the arrival date and spotting potential problems later on in the pregnancy. Your pregnant queen should be watched carefully, and kept away from stressful situations—this is not a good time to introduce a pet into the household or to remodel your house.

The queen's belly will not noticeably swell until after day 30, but the fetuses can be seen by use of ultrasonography (ultrasound) as early as day 14. The fetuses can also be felt by palpating the abdomen after day 16 or so, but this should only be done by a veterinarian as this can cause damage to the fetuses or to the uterus.

As the queen gets larger, her activity level will decrease. A certain amount of exercise is good for her, however. Allow her to play and to rest, as she chooses.

If you notice changes in your cat's health or any signs of illness, take her to the veterinarian immediately.

Normal gestation is 63 to 66 days but can be as early as 58 days (with greater kitten mortality) or as late as 71 days. A queen's gestation period will usually be the same, give or take a day of so, for each of her litters. Litters can run as high as eight kittens but the usual average is four or five.

Preparing for the Birth

As labor approaches, your queen will start to look for a nesting place. To avoid disagreements between you and your queen about the location of delivery, construct an appropriate nesting box for her and select a quiet birthing place. A large, sturdy cardboard box will work fine, although you can also purchase birthing boxes from pet supply stores. However, even the finest, most expensive birthing box won't dissuade your cat from delivering her kittens in the middle of your bed if she's determined to do so, so select a mutually agreeable place well in advance.

Your queen will want a place that's quiet, dark, and private. The birthing box should be large enough so the queen can stretch out comfortably on her side and high enough so she can stand, but not so big that's she's lost in it. It should have a lid that's removable so you can peek inside and an entrance that's high enough on the side of the box so the kittens won't tumble out. Line the box with cloth baby diapers, old sheets, or other bedding. Don't use your good sheets because the birth will be messy. Don't use terry cloth as that can snag the tiny claws of the kittens.

You can also place an electric heating pad, set at the lowest setting, underneath the other bedding, but be sure to leave an area of the box unheated so the kittens can move if they become too warm. Bedding should occupy about half of the box.

Put the birthing box in a quiet, out-of-the-way place and introduce it to your queen. Hopefully, she will accept it and she'll spend time in it each day, rearranging the contents and resting. If she doesn't like the box, it's probably because she doesn't like the location you've selected or it's too early for her to begin nesting. Try a different spot. Better yet, follow the queen around, see where she goes to establish a nest, and put the box in that location, if it's not too inconvenient (the inside of the dryer or your underwear drawer is out of the question).

During the last two weeks or so, the queen's body will look bumpy and you will probably be able to see the kittens moving from time to time. If you rest

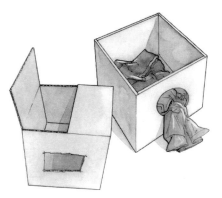

A nesting box can be made inexpensively using a cardboard box. Wooden or plastic nesting boxes can be purchased at pet supply stores. If you are planning more than one litter, a professional nesting box is a good investment.

your hand lightly on your queen's abdomen, you may feel the kittens moving. In the last week, her milk will start (you can tell by gently squeezing the nipple), and she may have contractions. This is normal.

At this point, you may need to assist the queen with grooming because she may be too large to clean herself properly after using the litter box. If this is the case, use moistened cotton balls to clean the vulva and anus. Gently pat the area dry with facial tissue.

The Normal Birth

When the queen reaches the last week of pregnancy, gather the supplies you will need to assist her. These are:
- small, blunt-tipped, unsharpened scissors
- gauze pads
- Betadine solution
- a notepad and pen or pencil
- wristwatch
- thin rubber gloves
- hemostatic forceps
- unwaxed dental floss
- a postage or diet scale (capable of measuring up to 2 pounds [0.9 kg] in 1-ounce [29 g] increments)
- a hot water bottle or heating pad
- your veterinarian's emergency phone number

Ruddy Abyssinian (left) and red Abyssinian (right).

You should let your veterinarian know that the birth is approaching and make arrangements for contacting him or her if there is a problem with the birth, even if the birth occurs in the early hours of the morning. An established relationship with an experienced breeder can be very helpful as well. Breeders often call each other with questions or problems during their cats' deliveries.

On the day of the labor, the queen's temperature will usually drop a point or two from the standard 102°F (38.9°C). When labor is approaching, the queen will seem restless, cry loudly, refuse to eat, lick her vulva, and may pass a bloody discharge. She probably will want you to stay with her as she rests in, or rearranges the contents of, her birthing box. She may also try to use the litter box without result, because she can confuse the pressure of approaching birth with the need to eliminate. When labor is imminent, she will take to her birthing box and stay there. When you know labor is approaching, scrub your hands thoroughly, and douse the scissors and the forceps in Betadine solution.

When the queen enters early labor (called stage-I labor), remain calm and stay with the queen and reassure her that everything is okay. Be prepared to stay with the queen until all kittens are delivered. Keep visitors to a minimum, avoid loud noises, keep your voice quiet, and avoid dashing about. Don't leave the queen alone to fend for herself—complications can arise that can threaten both mother and kittens.

When the placental "plug" enters the cervix, the queen experiences uterine contractions that start to push the kittens toward the vagina. Your cat's abdomen will bunch with each contraction. The contractions are slow and rhythmic; during this stage the cervix is softening and opening and the kittens are being moved down to the opening of the cervix. Time the contractions as they come, and record them in the notebook along with the relative intensity. Stage-I labor can last up to 24 hours but is usually less.

If the contractions do not strengthen and eventually cease, the labor was merely a false alarm. You must again wait (as patiently as any prospective "parent" can at a time like this).

In stage-II labor, the first fetus enters the birth canal and the contractions become more forceful. When the hard (bearing down) contractions begin, the queen will usually sit in a crouched position. With each contraction her abdomen heaves, her whiskers arch together in front of her face, and she may cry out and pant. The contractions should be coming at about two- to three-minute intervals and the contractions may come grouped together in twos or threes. Stage-II labor usually lasts about 30 minutes or so but can go longer.

When the first kitten is born and before the placenta (afterbirth) is delivered, the mother will remove the membrane (called the amniotic sac) surrounding the kitten and lick the kitten's face. Sometimes the membrane will burst during the birth process and only remnants will remain on the kitten.

The next group of contractions will usually deliver the placenta. The queen will eat the placentas (or some of them, at any rate). Allow her to do so, as the placenta contains hormones and nutrients that are good for her. Keep an eye on her, though. An inexperienced queen may not know where the placenta ends and the kitten begins.

If the kitten comes out part way and the next contractions do not push it out the rest of the way, you can help by smearing a little dab of petroleum jelly between the kitten and the vaginal wall to help the kitten slide free. Don't be alarmed if the kitten is presented rear

Fawn Abyssinian. Note the warm rose-beige coat ticked with light cocoa-brown. The fawn color is a dilution of red.

first as long as you can see both feet and the tail. Hind feet-first births account for about 50 percent of feline births and are not generally a problem. However, if the kitten is a true breech birth—if the hindquarters are presented but the legs are not visible—call your veterinarian right away.

Be sure to record each placenta as it is delivered. There should be one placenta per kitten. A retained placenta can cause infection and the death of the queen. However, *DO NOT* pull on the umbilical cord to dislodge the placenta. The placenta must come free on its own. If you rip the uterus by yanking on the placenta, your queen will die.

If the queen does not lick away the membrane, gently pinch the sac open and clean it from the kitten's face with a gauze pad. It's important to clean away the mucus and membrane quickly so the kitten can breathe.

The cord joining the kitten to the placenta will automatically constrict after blood has finished pumping into the kitten. This prevents the blood from exiting. You don't have to rush to cut the cord. The queen may do it for you anyway. However, the cord must be cut right away if the kitten is having trouble breathing, because you'll need

The queen licks her kittens to remove the birth sac and to stimulate circulation and respiration.

Kitten Development

Age	Development
10–20 days	eyes open
16–20 days	crawls
2–3 weeks	deciduous teeth appear
3 weeks	walks
3–4 weeks	eats first solid food
3–4 weeks	begin litter box training
5 weeks	register the kitten's pedigree
4–5 weeks	runs
4–5 weeks	washes self
4–5 weeks	begins to play
6-8 weeks	practices hunting skills
8 weeks	fully weaned
9 weeks	first shots
12 weeks	second shots
12 weeks	can go to new home
12 weeks	kitten's eye color changes
12–18 weeks	permanent teeth appear
24 weeks	total independence from mother
24–36 weeks	time to spay
36–52 weeks	time to neuter

to "sling" the kitten. You can't do that while the placenta is attached.

If the placenta hasn't been delivered after about five minutes or so, go ahead and cut the cord anyway. Clamp the cord with the forceps and, using dull scissors, cut the cord as close to the vulva of the mother as possible. Leave about 1 inch (2.5 cm) of the cord attached to the kitten. It's a mistake to cut the cord too short. Douse the cut end of the cord with Betadine solution to prevent infection. If the end of the cord continues to bleed, tie it with a piece of dental floss.

If the kitten makes choking or gurgling sounds (indications that fluids are present in the airways), "sling" the kitten by holding it between your hands with the head held between your fingertips. Swing downward gently to force the fluids from the kitten's lungs. Then wipe the kitten's nose and face again with a gauze pad. Rubbing the kitten with a towel will also stimulate the kitten to breathe.

Between each birth there is an interlude in which the queen rests, cleans, and nurses her kitten, and may even leave the box for a time. Allow her to do as she pleases. The interlude may be only 15 minutes or so, or it could be much longer. The entire litter is usually born in two to six hours, although a rare delivery will take several days. For each kitten, record the time of each birth, weight, gender, and when the placenta was delivered. The average size of an Abyssinian litter is three to four kittens; Abyssinians rarely have six or more to a litter. On average, a slightly higher percentage of male kittens are born than female kittens.

Complications of Delivery

If your queen has not produced her first kitten after an hour of hard contractions, it's time to call your veterinarian. If she partially delivers a kitten and then cannot seem to proceed, call the veterinarian. If she is bleeding bright red blood from her vagina, take her to the veterinarian immediately.

If a kitten is born that appears lifeless, don't give up on it immediately. It will sometimes revive if you briskly rub and stimulate it, warm it with a damp washcloth, raise and lower its arms, and blow gently into its mouth. If it feels cool to the touch, warm it by placing it on a warm water bottle, holding it into a pail of water heated to 101°F (38.3°C) (with, of course, the head of the kitten out of the water). You could also place it onto a heating pad set on the lowest setting.

Care of the Newborn

It's important for the kittens to nurse as soon as possible. The mother's first milk, colostrum, contains antibodies that give the kittens temporary immunity against diseases. The kittens, blind and deaf at birth, find their mother's nipples by smell and touch. If the kittens try to nurse and then cry, the mother's milk may not have come in. Gently squeeze the nipples to see if milk is produced. If she is dry, call the veterinarian immediately—sometimes the milk can be started with an injection of hormone.

Put the queen's litter box and food and water dishes nearby so she can stay with her kittens constantly. Keep visitors to a minimum for the first few days.

The tiny kittens will do nothing but sleep and eat for about the first ten days of their lives. Weigh each kitten daily. The kittens should be born weighing about 3.5 ounces (100 g) with a variance of 0.35 ounces or so (10 g) or so, and should gain about 0.35 ounces (10 g) each day. If any of the kittens does not gain weight or gains too slowly, that's a sign of trouble.

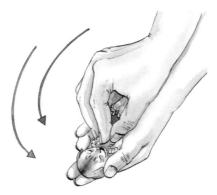

You can clear fluids from a kitten's respiratory passages by slinging.

Sometimes a queen will reject her kittens or will seem completely disinterested in them. If this happens, try putting her scent onto the kittens by rubbing them against the side of her mouth. If that doesn't work, try gently rubbing their genitals with a cloth to stimulate urination and then present the kitten's rear end to the mother. This will encourage the mother to clean the kitten, and that is usually enough to make her accept it.

If she refuses all efforts to make her care for the kittens, try to find a "foster

Kitten formula must be heated to 101°F (38.3°C) for feeding. Sterilize the bottle thoroughly between feedings.

Red and ruddy Abyssinian kittens (JT's Cattery) sitting still for a rare moment.

mother" for the kittens by calling your breeder or veterinarian. If you cannot find one, you will have to feed the kittens by hand. Use a Catac nurser (this curved nurser has a nipple the size and shape of the queen's) and kitten formula, both available at pet supply stores. If you can't find a Catac nurser, an eyedropper will also work well. It's very important to sterilize the nurser in between feedings to prevent the kittens' catching harmful bacteria or viruses. You can sterilize the nurser by immersing it in boiling water for 15 minutes.

Fostering is a grueling task, because you must get up every two hours without fail to feed the kittens. At each feeding you must also massage the kittens' anuses and genitals with a warm cloth to stimulate urination and defecation. If you don't, the kittens will die.

Development of the Kittens

After about ten days, the kittens' eyes open. It's very important for you to spend time with the developing kittens, handling them and playing with them. Kittens that are handled at a very young age will grow up to be better adjusted, friendlier, and more people-oriented cats than will kittens that have been ignored or shut away.

Spend time with the kittens each day. When they are old enough, allow them to investigate the house and spend time with the rest of the family. The future owners of the kittens will thank you for it, and you'll get to experience the product of all your hard work—the adorable, playful Abyssinian kittens.

Getting Abyssinian kittens to hold still for the camera takes skill and patience.

Showing Your Abyssinian

Cat Shows

If you haven't been to a cat show, you're in for a real treat. Nowhere else can you ogle exotic breeds, talk to breeders, judges, and enthusiasts, and see beautiful specimens of the cat breeds competing for awards. Not to mention the opportunity to shop till you drop for cat accessories, toys, and knickknacks. Cat shows are also great places to meet like-minded people and gather valuable information about your Abyssinian companion and cats in general. Even if you do not intend to show your cat, go to at least one or two shows, just for the experience.

Unless you live in a very out-of-the-way place, a cat show will be coming to your area soon. Check one of the cat magazines (see page 110) for a list of upcoming shows, or call the cat associations for information.

Cat Clubs

Although cats and humans have had a long history together, it was not until the mid 1800s that people began taking an interest in showing their cats and entering them into competition. Cat clubs formed to establish and promote specific pedigreed breeds, to share breeding and cat care information, and to further humanitarian causes.

Today the clubs keep stud records, draw up and record pedigrees, organize cat shows, provide information and training for breeders and judges, keep in touch with foreign cat associations, and feature lectures and publi-

cations geared toward the members. There are now seven cat-registering associations in North America.

The American Cat Association (ACA), formed in 1899, is the oldest U.S. cat organization. The Cat Fanciers' Association (CFA) is the largest today and has members as far away as Japan and Canada. CFA works closely with the Federation Internationale Feline (FIFe), a well-organized international organization that oversees European, North American, and Australian cat associations. The International Cat Association (TICA), formed in 1979, is the second largest registry in the United States, and has additional charters in Argentina, Brazil, Canada, France, Japan, the Philippines, Singapore, and Switzerland.

The First Cat Shows

Cats were exhibited as early as the 16th century, but the first cat show as such was held in 1871 at the Crystal Palace in Sydenham, London. This show was staged by Harrison Weir, a noted cat expert and cat fancier of the time, whom many people regard as the father of the cat fancy. ("Cat fancy" has become the common term used to describe the group of people interested in and involved with showing or breeding cats or belonging to a cat club.) The show featured 170 cats, including Weir's blue tabby (who won), Angoras, Persians, and Siamese, among others. The show was such a success that the showing of pedigreed

Getting your cat used to being held by strangers will help it adjust to being judged in the show ring.

cats suddenly became a popular activity in the United Kingdom—and one that continues today.

The first American all-breed cat show was held in 1895 in New York's Madison Square Garden. Other states followed suit, and soon the love of showing pedigreed cats spread through every state of the union. Today, there is at least one cat show held on most weekends of the year.

At first, cat shows were primarily a pastime of the rich and famous, or at least the well-known and well-to-do. Today the love of cats crosses every social, sexual, racial, and political barrier, and is popular over the entire globe. (I envision a new world order, where warring nations duke it out in the cat show arena—and the one with the best cats wins the war.)

How a Cat Show Works

Any pedigreed Abyssinian that is vaccinated, clean, healthy, and not declawed can compete in a cat show. An unpedigreed Abyssinian or a part-Abyssinian cat can be shown in the household pet category, where cats

are judged on their beauty and character rather than on the standard of a particular breed.

A particular cat association sponsors each show, usually in collaboration with one or more of the association's clubs. Some cat shows are for particular breeds only, some for longhairs or shorthairs, and some for all breeds.

Cats can be registered in one of three show classes: non-championship, championship, and alter (called premiership in the CFA). The nonchampionship classes are separated into five divisions: kitten class for cats not under four months but not yet eight months old; any other variety (AOV) class, designed for any pedigreed registered cat or kitten that qualifies for championship or alter competition but does not conform to the standard in color or coat; provisional breed class for breeds of cats not currently accepted for championship status but have a provisional standard approved; miscellaneous (non-competitive) class for breeds not accepted for provisional breed competition; and the household pet class for any domestic kitten or altered cat.

The championship divisions are divided into three classes: open class for unaltered cats of either gender that have not achieved championship status; champion class for cats that have attained championships; and grand champion class for cats that have attained grand championships.

The alter classes are for spayed or neutered cats that would, as whole cats, be eligible for championship status. These classes follow the same eligibility requirements as the championship classes.

Wins made in the championship classes are not transferable to the alter classes. If a champion cat is subsequently altered, it still retains its previously won titles. Make sure to enter the

The coat of the red Somali is warm, glowing red, ticked with chocolate brown. Note the luxurious tail.

cat in the right class; a cat registered in the wrong class can be disqualified.

In each show, two top awards are bestowed: best of breed (or best of color) to the finest example in each breed, and best of show to the most beautiful specimen of the entire exhibition.

Your Abyssinian's First Show

Showing an Abyssinian can be an exciting, fun-filled, and rewarding experience. It also can be expensive, exhausting, time-consuming, and disappointing if your beloved cat companion, who you think is beautiful beyond words, is not chosen by the judges.

Some people show their cats occasionally, whenever a cat show comes to town, and consider showing their cat a pleasing hobby where they meet with friends and "talk cat." Other exhibitors take showing their cats very seriously and make breeding, promoting, and advancing their cats their full-time jobs. Whatever style you choose, you will find like-minded associates in the show halls.

Before taking a cat to its first show, make the proper preparations. First, decide in which association or associations you wish to show. Your breeder will have provided a certificate of pedigree and a registration form for the association or associations of which he or she is a member. When you mail the registration form and fee to the association and receive proof of registration,

ZePunk enjoys spending time perched on a chair watching her favorite "TV" show—the birds in the backyard.

your cat is eligible for entry into that association's shows. Your breeder may be willing to guide you in the preparation of the paperwork for your first show. After all, the breeder wants to help you win—his or her cattery gains status by producing winning cats.

Next, send for a copy of the association's show rules and breed standard. For only a few dollars, this will provide a wealth of information on how to show your cat.

The closing date for entering is usually a month or more before the show, so allow plenty of time for the paperwork to be processed. If you elect to have someone show your cat for you, you must designate the person on the form in advance.

Because having the cat in peak condition is vitally important to winning, preparations must begin well in advance. Now's the time to pay special attention to the cat's diet, grooming, and mental readiness. Before the show, trim the cat's nails and groom it meticulously.

If your cat has never been shown, it's important to prepare it for the noise and bustle of the show hall and to accustom it to being handled by strangers. A cat that bites or scratches out of fear certainly won't make a good impression on the judge and may be disqualified. Well before the show, have friends come over and pretend to judge the cat. Have them hold it up, stretch it out, run a hand through its fur, wave a feather in front of its nose to test its reaction. Get the cat used to being penned, too, by keeping it caged for short periods at home. The cat will fare better if it's familiar with the process ahead of time.

Your first cat show may be a little overwhelming for both you and your cat. When you get to the cat show, your cat will be checked in, application forms and vaccination records will be verified, and a cage number will be assigned. After that, you can proceed to the show hall, where rows of benching cages await occupants. Commonly, the perimeter of the show hall is lined with judging rings, whereas row after row of benching cages crowd the center.

Sanitize the benching cage before putting your cat inside. Equip the cage with a litter box, water, food, a soft pillow for your cat to sit on, and any toys or accessories that will make the cat feel at home. Decorate the cage if you wish, and then give your cat a final grooming to prepare it for judging.

When your cat's number is called, you will take the cat to the judging ring, where you will place your cat in a cage to await judging. Now comes the hard part—watching your cat being judged, hoping it behaves, and waiting to see if a winning ribbon will be hung on its cage. Will your cat bring home a rosette? You'll never know unless you try!

CFA Abyssinian Show Standard

General: the overall impression of the ideal Abyssinian would be a colorful cat with a distinctly ticked coat, medium in size, and regal in appearance. The Abyssinian is lithe, hard, and muscular, showing eager activity and a lively interest in all surroundings. Well-balanced temperamentally and physically with all elements of the cat in proportion.

Head: a modified, slightly rounded wedge without flat planes; the brow,

CFA Point	Score
Head (25)	
Muzzle	6
Skull	6
Ears	7
Eye Shape	6
Body (30)	
Torso	15
Legs and Feet	10
Tail	5
Coat (10)	
Texture	10
Color (35)	
Color	15
Ticking	15
Eye Color	5
Total	100

cheek, and profile lines all showing a gentle contour. A slight rise from the bridge of the nose to the forehead, which should be of good size, with width between the ears and flowing into the arched neck without a break.

Muzzle: not sharply pointed or square. The chin should be neither receding nor protruding. Allowance should be made for jowls in adult males.

Ears: alert, large, and moderately pointed; broad, and cupped at base and set as though listening. Hair on ears very short and close lying, preferably tipped with black or dark brown on a ruddy Abyssinian, chocolate-brown on a red Abyssinian, slate blue on the blue Abyssinian, or light cocoa brown on a fawn Abyssinian.

Eyes: almond-shaped, large, brilliant, and expressive. Neither round nor oriental. Eyes accentuated by fine dark line, encircled by light-colored area.

Body: medium long, lithe, and graceful, but showing well-developed muscular strength without coarseness.

Abyssinian conformation strikes a medium between the extremes of the cobby and the svelte lengthy type. Proportion and general balance more to be desired than mere size.

Legs and Feet: proportionately slim, fine-boned. The Abyssinian stands well off the ground giving the impression of being on tip-toe. Paw small, oval, and compact.

Toes: five in front and four behind.

Tail: thick at base, fairly long and tapering.

Coat: soft, silky, fine in texture, but dense and resilient to the touch with a lustrous sheen. Medium in length but long enough to accommodate two or three dark bands of ticking.

Penalize: off-color pads. Long narrow head, short round head. Barring on legs, dark broken necklace markings, rings on tail. Coldness or gray tones in the coat.

Disqualify: white locket, or white anywhere other than nostril, chin, and upper throat area. Kinked or abnormal tail. Dark unbroken necklace. Gray undercoat close to the skin extending throughout a major portion of the body. Any black hair on red Abyssinian. Incorrect number of toes. Any color other than the four accepted colors.

Abyssinian Colors

Coat Color: warm and glowing. Ticking: distinct and even, with dark-colored bands contrasting with lighter-colored bands on the hair shafts. Undercoat color clear and bright to the skin. Deeper color shades desired, however intensity of ticking not to be sacrificed for depth of color. Darker shading along spine allowed if fully ticked. Preference given to cats UNMARKED on the undersides, chest, and legs; tail without rings. *Facial Markings*: dark lines extending from eyes and brows, cheekbone shading, dots and shad-

ing on whisker pads are all desirable enhancements. Eyes accentuated by fine dark line, encircled by light colored area. *Eye color*: gold or green, the more richness and depth of color the better.

Ruddy: coat ruddy brown (burnt-sienna), ticked with various shades of darker brown or black; the extreme outer tip to be the darkest, with orange-brown undercoat. Tail tipped with black. The underside and inside of legs to be a tint to harmonize with the main color. *Nose leather*: tile red. *Paw pads*: black or brown, with black between toes, extending slightly beyond the paws.

Red: coat rich, warm glowing red, ticked with chocolate-brown, the extreme outer tip to be dark, with red undercoat. Tail tipped with chocolate-brown. The underside and inside of legs to be a tint to harmonize with the main color. *Nose leather*: rosy pink. *Paw pads*: pink, with chocolate-brown between toes, extending slightly beyond the paws.

Blue: coat warm beige, ticked with various shades of slate blue, the extreme outer tip to be the darkest, with blush beige undercoat. Tail tipped with slate blue. The underside and inside of legs to be a tint to harmonize with the main color. *Nose leather*: old rose. *Paw pads*: mauve, with slate blue between toes, extending slightly beyond the paws.

Fawn: coat warm rose-beige, ticked with light cocoa brown, the extreme outer tip to be the darkest, with blush beige undercoat. Tail tipped with light cocoa brown. The underside and inside of legs to be a tint to harmonize with the main color. *Nose leather*: salmon. *Paw pads*: pink with light cocoa brown between the toes, extending slightly beyond the paws.

Abyssinian allowable outcross breeds: none.

Source: The Cat Fanciers' Association

Phenotype Color Inheritance Chart

	Pure Ruddy	Ruddy c/Blue	Ruddy c/Red	Ruddy c/Red & Blue	Pure Blue	Blue c/Red	Pure Red	Red c/Blue
Pure Ruddy	100% Ruddy	100% Ruddy	100% Ruddy	100% Ruddy	100% Ruddy	100% Ruddy	100% Ruddy	100% Ruddy
Ruddy c/Blue	100% Ruddy	75% Ruddy 25% Blue	100% Ruddy	75% Ruddy 25% Blue	50% Ruddy 50% Blue	50% Ruddy 50% Blue	100% Ruddy	75% Ruddy 25% Blue
Ruddy c/Red	100% Ruddy	100% Ruddy	75% Ruddy 25% Red	75% Ruddy 25% Red	100% Ruddy	75% Ruddy 25% Red	50% Ruddy 50% Red	50% Ruddy 50% Red
Ruddy c/Red & Blue	100% Ruddy	75% Ruddy 25% Blue	75% Ruddy 25% Red	56.25% Ruddy 18.75% Blue 18.75% Red 6.25% Fawn	50% Ruddy 50% Blue	37.5% Ruddy 37.5% Blue 12.5% Red 12.5% Fawn	50% Ruddy 50% Red	37.5% Ruddy 12.5% Blue 37.5% Red 12.5% Fawn
Pure Blue	100% Ruddy	50% Ruddy 50% Blue	100% Ruddy	50% Ruddy 50% Blue	100% Blue	100% Blue	100% Ruddy	50% Ruddy 50% Blue
Blue c/Red	100% Ruddy	50% Ruddy 50% Blue	75% Ruddy 25% Red	37.5% Ruddy 37.5% Blue 12.5% Red 12.5% Fawn	100% Blue	75% Blue 25% Fawn	50% Ruddy 50% Red	25% Ruddy 25% Blue 25% Red 25% Fawn
Pure Red	100% Ruddy	100% Ruddy	50% Ruddy 50% Red	50% Ruddy 50% Red	100% Ruddy	50% Ruddy 50% Red	100% Red	100% Red
Red c/Blue	100% Ruddy	75% Ruddy 25% Blue	50% Ruddy 50% Red	37.5% Ruddy 12.5% Blue 37.5% Red 12.5% Fawn	50% Ruddy 50% Blue	25% Ruddy 25% Blue 25% Red 25% Fawn	100% Red	75% Red 25% Fawn

Ruddy Abyssinian.

Key:

c/ = Carrying

P = Pure

R = Red

B = Blue

R&B = Red and Blue

Useful Addresses and Literature

American and Canadian Cat Associations

American Association of Cat
Enthusiasts (AACE)
P.O. Box 213
Pine Brook, NJ 07058
(201) 335-6717

American Cat Association (ACA)
Dept. CF
8101 Katherine Avenue
Panorama City, CA 91402
(818) 781-5656

American Cat Fanciers
Association (ACFA)
Dept. CF
P.O. Box 203
Pt. Lookout, MO 65726
(417) 334-5430

Canadian Cat Association (CCA)
Dept. CF
83 Kennedy Road, Unit 1806
Brampton, Ontario
Canada L6W 3P3

Cat Fanciers' Association (CFA)
Dept. CF
1805 Atlantic Avenue
P.O. Box 1005
Manasquan, NJ 08736
(908) 528-9797

Cat Fanciers Federation (CFF)
Dept. CF
9509 Montgomery Road
Cincinnati, OH 45242
(513) 984-1841

The International Cat
Association (TICA)
Dept. CF
P.O. Box 2684
Harlingen, TX 78551
(210) 428-8046

Abyssinian and Somali Cat Clubs

Abyssinian Cat Club of America
4060 Croaker Lane
Woodbridge, VA 22193

The Grand Somali Society
238 Church Street
Poughkeepsie, NY 12601

Somali Cat Club
10 Western Boulevard
Gillette, NJ 07933

Somali Cat Club of America Inc.
5027 Armstrong
Wichita, KS 67204

Other Organizations, Foundations, and Animal Protection Agencies

American Humane Association
P.O. Box 1266
Denver, CO 80201
(303) 695-0811

American Society for the
Prevention of Cruelty to
Animals (ASPCA)
424 East 92nd Street
New York, NY 10128
(212) 876-7700

Cornell Feline Health Center
New York State College of
Veterinary Medicine
Cornell University
Ithaca, NY 14853

The Delta Society
P.O. Box 1080
Renton, WA 98057
(206) 226-7357

Friends of Animals
P.O. Box 1244
Norwalk, CT 06856
(800) 631-2212
(for low cost spay/neuter
program information)

Fund for Animals
200 W. 57th Street
New York, NY 10019
(212) 246-2096

The Humane Society of the
United States (HSUS)
2100 L St. N.W.
Washington, DC 20037
(202) 452-1100

Pets Are Wonderful Support
(PAWS)
P.O. Box 460489
San Francisco, CA 94146
(415) 241-1460
(Provides pet-related services
for people with AIDS)

4 x 10/81   5 3/03

Robert H. Winn Foundation for
Cat Health
1805 Atlantic Avenue
P.O. Box 1005
Manasquan, NJ 08736-1005

Cat Magazines
Cats
Subscription information:
P.O. Box 420240
Palm Coast, FL 32142-0240
(904) 445-2818
Editorial offices:
P.O. Box 290037
Port Orange, FL 32129-0037
(904) 788-2770

Cat Fancy
Subscription information:
P.O. Box 52864
Boulder, CO 52864
Editorial offices:
P.O. Box 6050
Mission Viejo, CA 92690
(714) 855-8822

Cat Fancier's Almanac
Cat Fanciers' Association
Subscription information and
editorial offices:
1805 Atlantic Avenue
P.O. Box 1005
Manasquan, NJ 08736-0805
(908) 528-9797

Catnip (newsletter)
Tufts University School of
Veterinary Medicine

Subscription information:
P.O. Box 420014
Palm Coast, FL 32142-0014
(800) 829-0926
Editorial offices:
203 Harrison Avenue
Boston, MA 02111

Cat World
Subscription information and
editorial offices:
10 Western Road
Shoreham-By-Sea
West Sussex, BN43 5WD
England

I Love Cats
Subscription information:
P.O. Box 7013
Red Oak, IA 51591-0013
Editorial offices:
950 3rd Avenue, 16th Floor
New York, NY 10022-2705
(212) 888-1855

Books for Additional Reading

Behrend, Katrin. *Apartment Cats*. Barron's Educational Series, Inc., Hauppauge, New York: 1995.

Behrend, K. and Wegler, Monika. *The Complete Book of Cat Care*. Barron's Educational Series, Inc., Hauppauge, New York: 1991.

Carlson, Delbert G., D.V.M., and Giffin, James M., M.D. *Cat Owner's Veterinary Handbook*. Howell Book House, New York: 1983.

Daly, Carol Himsel, D.V.M. *Caring for Your Sick Cat*. Barron's Educational Series, Inc., Hauppauge, New York: 1994.

Frye, Fredric. *First Aid for Your Cat*. Barron's Educational Series, Inc., Hauppauge, New York: 1987.

Pedersen, Niels C. *Feline Husbandry*. American Veterinary Publications, Inc., Goleta, California: 1991.

Robinson, Roy. *Genetics for Cat Breeders*. Pergamon Press, Oxford: 1977.

Siegal, Mordecai and Cornell University. *The Cornell Book of Cats*. Villard Books, New York: 1989.

Viner, Bradley, D.V.M. *The Cat Care Manual*. Barron's Educational Series, Inc., Hauppauge, New York: 1993.

Wright, M. and S., Walters, eds. *The Book of the Cat*. Summit Books, New York: 1980.

Index